ASTD
Learning
System
User's Guide

ASTD Press is an internationally renowned source of insightful and practical information on workplace learning and performance topics, including training basics, evaluation and return-on-investment (ROI), instructional systems development (ISD), e-learning, leadership, and career development.

Ordering information: This ASTD Learning System and other books published by ASTD Press can be purchased by visiting our website at store.astd.org or by calling 800.628.2783 or 703.683.8100.

Library of Congress Control Number: 2006920965

ISBN-10: 1-56286-448-3

ISBN-13: 978-1-56286-448-4

ASTD Press Staff
Director: Cat Russo
Manager: Mark Morrow
Associate Editor: Tora Estep
Associate Editor: Jennifer Mitchell
Circulation Manager: Marnee Beck
Editorial Assistant: Kelly Norris
Bookstores and Inventory: Nancy Silva
Marketing Manager: Greg Akroyd
Production Coordinator: Rachel Beuter
Cover Design: Alizah Epstein

Table of Contents

1
Introduction

Welcome to the *ASTD Learning System*! This User's Guide will help explain everything you need to know to use this product to its best advantage. Chapters two through four provide an overview of the Certified Professional in Learning and Performance™ (CPLP) certification program and testing process. The remaining chapters and appendixes explain the purpose and use of the *ASTD Learning System*, with examples from the text, study tips, and preparation readiness assessment.

Based on the *ASTD Competency Study: Mapping the Future* (2004), an independent group of subject matter experts developed a content outline. It is from that outline that the *ASTD Learning System*, as well as the CPLP exam test items, was developed. The *ASTD Learning System* and the ASTD Certification Institute's CPLP exam were created completely independently of one another. Therefore, while the body of knowledge is present in the content of this study tool, it does not refer directly to the exam. As with all study materials, this product neither teaches to the test, nor guarantees you will pass.

The *ASTD Learning System* provides an academic body of knowledge—it is not meant for on-the-job application. It is important to keep in mind that its purpose is to aquire knowledge, and to assess those areas that require extra attention. The *ASTD Learning System* will help bridge the gap between experience and knowledge. Other resources provide valuable practical application.

The *ASTD Learning System* content was developed by instructional designers at Thomson NetG and ASTD staff editors. The content presented here combines classic theories with some of the most current information and applications available. The development team used a variety of resources to compile, write, and edit this information, including ASTD Press books, *Infolines*, case studies, journal articles, websites, and numerous prominent works on workplace learning and performance (WLP). The master reference list can be found in Appendix E of Module 7: *Coaching*.

This is ASTD Press's first edition of the *ASTD Learning System*. The WLP field and the body of knowledge are evolutionary, and the *ASTD Learning System* aligns to the competency model developed in 2004. While the profession continues to develop and grow, so will ASTD Press continue to provide revised versions of the *ASTD Learning System,* featuring the most up-to-date information possible.

Figure 1-1. The ASTD Competency Model

The ASTD Competency Model

SUCCESSFUL EXECUTION
FOCUS
FOUNDATION

=
+

learning strategist

business partner

project manager

professional specialist

WORKPLACE LEARNING AND PERFORMANCE ROLES

DESIGNING LEARNING
IMPROVING HUMAN PERFORMANCE
DELIVERING TRAINING
MEASURING AND EVALUATING
FACILITATING ORGANIZATIONAL CHANGE
MANAGING THE LEARNING FUNCTION
COACHING
MANAGING ORGANIZATIONAL KNOWLEDGE
CAREER PLANNING AND TALENT MANAGEMENT

AREAS OF EXPERTISE : SUPPORTED BY TECHNOLOGY

● INTERPERSONAL
> Building Trust
> Communicating Effectively
> Influencing Stakeholders
> Leveraging Diversity
> Networking and Partnering

● BUSINESS / MANAGEMENT
> Analyzing Needs and Proposing Solutions
> Applying Business Acumen
> Driving Results
> Planning and Implementing Assignments
> Thinking Strategically

● PERSONAL
> Demonstrating Adaptability
> Modeling Personal Development

COMPETENCIES . COMPETENCIES . COMPETENCIES

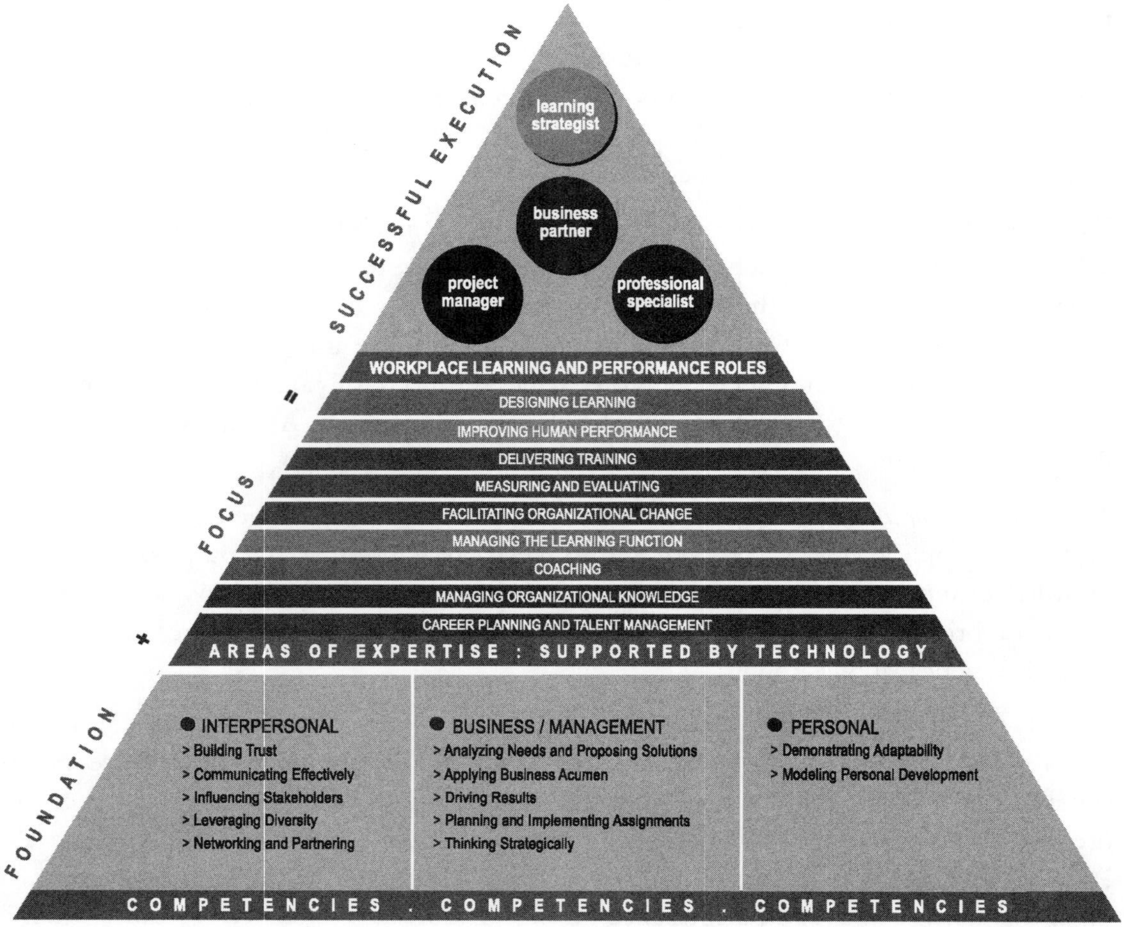

Overview of Modules

The following are brief descriptions of each module of the *ASTD Learning System*. For more information on the *ASTD Competency Study: Mapping the Future*, see Chapter 2, "CPLP." A comprehensive content list for each individual module is in Appendix A.

Module 1: *Designing Learning*

This module focuses on an understanding of the foundational theories and concepts of adult learning as well as the array of instructional methods available for designing learning. In addition, this module addresses various methods to consider when designing learning solutions, as well as needs assessment, acquisition of core content to be taught, and the need to be adept at researching topics to create effective instruction. Designing, creating, and developing effective learning and training that meets the needs of participants are the basic elements of this study module. How technology affects instructional design is also important, and must be maximized to create effective training.

Module 2: *Delivering Training*

This module centers on the many different avenues of training delivery available. The WLP professional should be comfortable identifying each avenue's characteristics, value, and applicability to learning, classroom, blended, and multimedia delivery. A fundamental understanding of the basics of adult learning theory combined with these delivery techniques and tools are required. From a testing perspective, the WLP professional must be knowledgeable in the training delivery styles, recognizing learning styles and instructor learning preferences to maintain flexibility within a training program. The WLP professional must also be able to distinguish between an organizational learning need and individual learner needs and styles.

Module 3: *Improving Human Performance*

CPLP exam preparation for the field of human performance improvement (HPI) includes data gathering, analysis, change management, and measurement. The WLP practitioner must be able to articulate internal and external elements that affect systems and contribute to the success of an HPI initiative. Knowledge and identification of the various HPI models is required. Exploring current culture, understanding desired performance and business goals, and maintaining a neutral mindset without preconceived solutions are critical to the success of any HPI initiative. The WLP practitioner needs to demonstrate expertise in collecting data; asking the right questions; determining needs and conducting analyses; dealing with people; and understanding behavioral styles and personalities, organizational cultures, and group facilitation strategies.

Module 4: *Measuring and Evaluating*

This module's core focus is a foundational understanding and knowledge of the measurement and evaluation methods and metrics available to the WLP professional. A basic understanding of statistics and data collection, as well as research methodology, is crucial to attaining a full level of comprehension of the material covered. Knowledge of systematic approaches to evaluation and various evaluation methodologies, design of research methods to implement measurement and evaluation activities, assessment of proposed methods, and recommendations on how to implement a measurement and evaluation activity are required. It is also important for the WLP practitioner to understand the value of learning and performance solutions, ways to focus individual programs and create overall measures of system effectiveness, and methods of leveraging findings to increase value and propose change initiatives. The ability to analyze existing business processes and procedures to determine overall organizational health is also needed.

Module 5: *Facilitating Organizational Change*

A foundational knowledge of change theories is essential to help organizations successfully navigate and facilitate change. The WLP professional must understand organizational culture in its broadest sense and its manifestations in the day-to-day interactions of employees, engaging others to actively participate in the identification, solution, and assessment of problems and issues. Knowledge of motivating factors is critical when implementing organizational change to minimize resistance, turnover, and failure to institutionalize change. From a testing preparation perspective, the WLP professional must be aware of the various change models and theories used by organizations: motivation theory; engagement practices; communications models and theories; process design; and organizational systems and theories, including appreciative inquiry, action research, and systems thinking.

Module 6: *Managing the Learning Function*

The WLP professional needs a core understanding of how the learning function affects all areas of an organization, as well as the core competencies involved with managing learning within an organization. An important element is knowledge of the business drivers of an organization, which the learning function can then best support organizational goals and objectives. Knowledge of the various learning technologies that are available and their use in the learning function is critical for success of any program. WLP professionals should be aware of how human resource systems integrate into the success of the training function, as well as external systems and laws or regulations that shape the culture of an organization and affect business trends. Fundamentals include legal and ethical requirements, models and concepts of adult learning, administration of programs, project management, strategic planning, budgeting and financial acumen, learning management systems, and knowledge of marketplace resources to assist in the management of learning.

Module 7: *Coaching*

This module covers the core elements required in the field of coaching to improve performance. Coaching involves using an interactive process to help individuals and organizations develop and produce results. Knowledge of core coaching competencies and standards is required. Factors such as the organizational culture and structure, available resources, and ways that organizational business objectives affect coaching programs need to be understood.

Module 8: *Managing Organizational Knowledge*

Understanding and comprehension of the foundational elements of knowledge management (KM) for the WLP professional is the focus of this module. KM involves the effective capture, use, and reuse of organizational knowledge to benefit the organization and individuals; it is especially through technology that the use of new and shared knowledge enables improvement. Awareness of the historical perspectives and best practices of KM;

primary business processes, drivers, and analysis; information architecture and database management; systems analysis and design; after action review methodology; and how these elements help the WLP practitioner prepare learning goals and plans is required. In addition, acquaintance with the various KM tools and technologies that are available, including knowledge mapping, need to be considered.

Module 9: *Career Planning and Talent Management*

This module covers information for the WLP professional relative to individual career planning and organizational talent management. The WLP professional should be aware of the workforce planning process, its implementation, and its outcomes at each step, ensuring that employees have the right skills to meet the strategic challenges of the organization. From a testing perspective, knowledge of other related human resource functions, such as diversity, employee relations, succession planning, job analysis, defining and communicating effective evaluation methods, and related supervisory skills are required. WLP professionals must be familiar with interviewing, counseling, producing or interpreting reports based on various psychological instruments, and assisting individuals in developing realistic career plans.

2
CPLP

The ASTD Certification Institute (CI) embarked on building the CPLP credential as a direct result of ASTD member demand. Members were clamoring for a way to prove their value. However, there are many other stakeholders besides ASTD members. The credential benefits

- *the profession*—by codifying it, creating standards, and positioning it for new heights

- *individuals*—by offering a means for ASTD members and nonmembers to prove their value and identifying a path for continued professional development

- *employers*—by providing a common reference point to help evaluate job candidates.

What the CPLP Covers

Receiving the CPLP credential signifies that you have a baseline knowledge in the following nine AOEs:

1. Designing Learning
2. Delivering Training
3. Improving Human Performance
4. Measuring and Evaluating
5. Facilitating Organizational Change
6. Managing the Learning Function
7. Coaching
8. Managing Organizational Knowledge
9. Career Planning and Talent Management.

These nine areas are identified in ASTD's latest competency model, which defines the clusters of skills, knowledge, abilities, and behaviors required for success across all WLP jobs.

The ASTD Competency Model (Figure 1-1), which is shaped like a pyramid, has three tiers: foundational competencies, AOEs, and WLP roles. The middle tier of the model illustrates the nine AOEs that form the basis for the CPLP. The AOEs are the specific technical and professional knowledge and skills required for success in the field.

Each AOE represents a distinct area of practice with unique outputs and knowledge areas, and each assumes the use of certain methods and operating processes. AOEs are the knowledge and skills an individual must have above and beyond the foundational competencies (the bottom tier). To function effectively in a given AOE, a person must display a blend of the appropriate foundational competencies and unique technical or professional skills and knowledge.

Self-Assessment

Before you begin to study for the exam, take the readiness assessment provided in Appendix B of this User's Guide. Doing so will help you determine where you need to focus your time.

As you think about committing to the CPLP, begin by asking yourself some important questions:

- What are my career goals and does certification align with them?

- How should I focus my professional development efforts?

- What is the gap between my knowledge and experience and certification program demands?

- Do I have the resources required—time, money, and commitment—to invest in the program?

Understand Your Career Goals

The CPLP is not the solution for everyone. What are the career goals that the CPLP can help satisfy? The CPLP is ideal for addressing career deficiencies that involve increasing and proving your skills and qualifications across the broad WLP field as well as to help you update or refresh your technical knowledge.

Understand Your Options

Certification indicates that you have met predetermined standards through testing. However, it does not guarantee competence for a specific job title in a particular company. Note also that certification is *not* a certificate. *Certificate* programs typically result in a document that signifies completion of a course or learning experience. Certification, by contrast, is more about testing and requires that you have had a certain amount of experience before you are eligible to join the program.

Determining whether to pursue a degree, a certificate, or certification is personal. The reasons why individuals seek out one versus another are not clear cut, so here are some to consider:

- *A degree* is awarded for intellectual development and covers the general knowledge required for a particular field.

- *A certificate* focuses on acquiring specific knowledge and skills during a learning event and has no testing requirement.

- *Certification* focuses on testing and providing evidence that signifies someone has the requisite knowledge and experience and has met predetermined standards to practice in the field.

The best choice depends on your goals and objectives and your employers' needs. Sometimes one or a combination of options is the best solution. Ultimately, the ideal path depends on your given situation as well as the amount of time, energy, and money you have to spend on its pursuit.

Develop a Realistic View of CPLP Certification

It is extremely important that you have a realistic picture of the CPLP prior to committing to the program. The CPLP can be a vital part of your career strategy, but is not the only part or even the most important part. Certification provides no guarantee of career success, or instant promotions or raises. It is not a one-time event; you must continue to learn and grow to keep your skills sharp and maintain your credentials. It takes a combination of experience, dedication, and hard work over the long haul to maintain certification and to ensure general career success.

Here are some common pitfalls and misconceptions to avoid:

Inadequate knowledge of the certification itself. Do not choose the CPLP just because it is popular. Read and understand the materials that describe what it involves and its objectives. An incomplete picture of what certification is about can lead to unrealistic expectations and disappointment.

Underestimation of the real costs of certification. You should not only include the cost of the test and the learning materials into the equation, but also include the drive required to finish it. How will you handle certification when you have conflicting commitments? What's in place to prevent you from cramming instead of mastering the material?

Inadequate knowledge and experience to sit for the exam. Assess honestly whether you meet eligibility requirements and have adequate knowledge and a realistic picture of the CPLP prior to committing to the program. Table 2-1 can help you determine your knowledge and experience level as it relates to the AOEs being tested, the gaps, and potential strategies you can use to close the gaps to prepare for the test.

Incomplete understanding of program requirements. It is important that you examine the certification requirements carefully. Read the materials available on the ASTD certification website to familiarize yourself with the program. Here are some examples of what you might want to investigate and understand at the onset:

- eligibility requirements
- monetary cost (including the learning materials and testing fees)
- study materials available
- time required
- retake policy
- your work history relative to AOEs (for Work Product submission)
- certification maintenance policy.

Use the chart below (Table 2-1) to help you determine your overall readiness for CPLP and then make use of the self-assessment by AOE in Appendix B to help you prepare for the knowledge-based portion of the CPLP exam.

Table 2-1. CPLP Readiness

Status	Eligibility	Breadth of Knowledge	Work Product	Fit	Commitment	Requirements
Ready to test	Meets minimum requirement of three years related experience*	Has had exposure to multiple areas of expertise	Has a Work Product to submit	CPLP fits in with career goals	Willing to spend resources (study time, money, etc.) required for CPLP	Have read and understood CPLP program requirements
Not ready to test	Does not meet minimum eligibility requirement	Has had limited or no exposure to AOEs	Does not have Work Product to submit	CPLP does not fit with career goals at the current time	Does not currently have resources required	Does not fully understand the CPLP program requirements

*This is a minimum eligibility requirement. If you meet this requirement, you should still carefully assess whether or not you are ready to take the exam.

Understand the Eligibility Requirements

To be eligible for CPLP certification, you must demonstrate that you have three years of work experience. You should provide accurate information about eligibility when you apply and register for CPLP certification. If you are found ineligible, you will not be accepted and must reapply during the next test window. So, it is in your best interest to ensure that your application provides factual information that meets eligibility requirements.

Understand the Certification Process

Now that you have a realistic view of certification, you're ready to look at what you'll have to accomplish to earn your CPLP designation. To become CPLP certified, you must

- have a *minimum* of **three years** work-related experience
- take and pass a knowledge-based exam that covers the nine AOEs
- submit a successful Work Product in one of the AOEs.

To simplify the process, here's an easy-to-follow breakdown of all of the steps involved (see Figure 2-1):

1. Assess your eligibility, professional goals, and program fit.

2. Enroll in the program through ASTD CI if there is a match.

3. Receive authorization to take the exam and schedule your exam.

4. Begin preparing for the knowledge-based exam.

5. Sit for, complete, and pass the knowledge-based exam.

6. Begin preparing the Work Product submission in one of the designated AOEs.

7. Submit your Work Product for review.

8. Receive a passing score on your Work Product submission.

9. Receive the CPLP designation. Maintain certification credits and recertify periodically, as required.

Figure 2-1. Steps to Becoming a Certified Professional in Learning and Performance (CPLP)

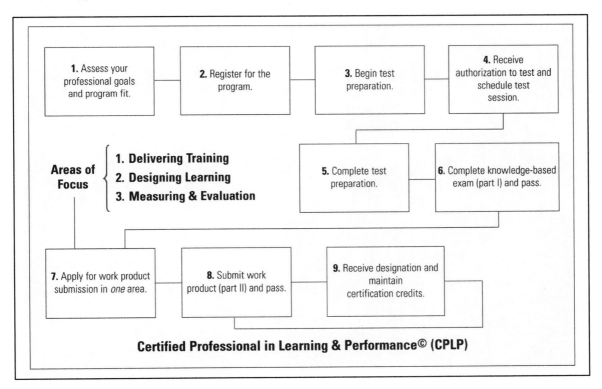

For More Information

For more information on the certification process including Candidate Bulletins, testing locations, dates and times, and exam details, including how it is scored and the fees involved, go to http://www.astd.org/astd/cplp or send an email to certification@astd.org.

3
The Knowledge-Based Exam

The CPLP exam contains 150 multiple-choice questions and focuses on breadth of knowledge across the AOEs. Each question is worth one point. You can skip a question if you do not know the answer, although we recommend that you make an educated guess rather than skip the question in its entirety because there is no penalty for guessing.

Questions derive more from certain AOEs than others, as shown in Table 3-1.

Table 3-1. Weighting by AOE

Topic	Exam Weighting (%)
1. Designing Learning	15
2. Delivering Training	15
3. Improving Human Performance	15
4. Measuring and Evaluating	12
5. Facilitating Organizational Change	12
6. Managing the Learning Function	9
7. Coaching	8
8. Managing Organizational Knowledge	8
9. Career Planning and Talent Management	6

Exam Content Outline

As stated in Chapter 1, the content outline that was developed by an independent group of subject matter experts and was derived, in part, from *The ASTD Competency Study: Mapping the Future* (ASTD, 2004). This content outline determines the topics that are covered on the exam. Table 3-2 provides an example of a knowledge area from AOE2: *Delivering Training*, and explains the function of each component of the content outline.

Table 3-2: Content Outline Sample

Sample Section	Components
AOE2-K9. Individual Learning Styles	This is identified as a key knowledge area by ASTD's competency research.
A learning style represents how a learner acquires knowledge or changes behavior. Each learner is motivated differently based on environment, psychological comfort, social styles, and profiles. Facilitators must understand and apply techniques that recognize all learning styles, or they will struggle in the classroom.	Each content paragraph explains how the WLP professional incorporates this key knowledge in his or her work. It suggests the depth level in the key knowledge area needed for certification.
A. visual, auditory, and kinesthetic (VAK) model B. David Kolb's four basic learning styles C. Harvey Silver and Robert Hanson's learning style inventory (based on Myers-Briggs) D. Howard Gardner's multiple intelligences (seven intelligences) E. Ned Herrmann's creative brain: brain-based approaches to learning F. perceptual modality G. factors affecting the speed at which adults learn (psychological, mental, and emotional characteristics of adult learning) H. Patricia Cross's adult learning (CAL and COR) I. accelerated learning techniques	Subject matter experts (SMEs) listed details in each key knowledge area identified. This list is meant to provide scope. In this example, you are not expected to know every model in great detail or who invented the model. Names are merely provided as a convenience. Often key knowledge crosses over different AOEs. When this occurs, you will be referred to the detailed information provided in another AOE.

Now let's take a closer look at a sample of one of the AOEs from the content outline.

AOE 1. Designing Learning

Designing, creating, and developing learning interventions to meet needs; analyzing and selecting the most appropriate strategy, methodologies, and technologies to maximize the learning experience and impact.

AOE1-K1. Cognition and Adult Learning Theory

As a WLP professional, you must understand theories and concepts of adult learning. When designing interventions for adults, you must identify characteristics and issues specific to that population to create effective instruction. A theory's or model's relevance to adult learning is more important than the theory's or model's originator(s).

- **A.** four theories of learning and instruction
- **B.** Abraham Maslow's hierarchy of needs
- **C.** Malcolm Knowles's adult learning theory, or andragogy
- **D.** differences between teaching and facilitating learning
- **E.** guidelines for facilitating learning (Carl Rogers)
- **F.** individual characteristics of learning
- **G.** adult development theories
- **H.** theories of learning and memory (how people learn and retain information)
- **I.** the learning brain model
- **J.** modes of learning
- **K.** external and environmental influences
- **L.** multiple intelligences (Howard Gardner)
- **M.** role of adult learning theories

AOE1-K2. Instructional Design Theory and Process

When designing instruction, you've most likely used many theories and models. Central to all of them is analysis, design, development, implementation, and evaluation of instruction. The models also include goals and objectives for instruction and assessment.

- **A.** theories and models for designing instruction
- **B.** goals and objectives
- **C.** basics of how courses are designed

AOE1-K3. Various Instructional Methods

To create an effective learning opportunity, a WLP professional must consider an array of instructional methods. Time, distance, budget, and schedules are a few issues you must consider when identifying appropriate formats. Instructional strategies must meet your participants' needs and create an effective learning atmosphere.

- **A.** active training techniques
- **B.** e-learning techniques
- **C.** ways to choose techniques

AOE1-K4. Various Training Delivery Options or Media

Performance improvement can require many methods and a broad variety of media. Classroom training can occur with all participants in the same room, or in rooms scattered around the world utilizing web cams. You must understand what is possible and when a specific medium is most effective.

- **A.** online learning
- **B.** electronic performance support system (EPSS)
- **C.** classroom training (face-to-face)
- **D.** blended learning
- **E.** electronic learning
- **F.** correspondence
- **G.** self-study

Sample Test Questions

These 10 questions are similar in format and content to the questions on the CPLP knowledge-based exam. These questions are intended to allow you to become familiar with the way the questions are asked and to give you an idea of the level of difficulty on the exam.

1. What type of sampling is used when every member of the population has an equal chance of selection? (Measuring and Evaluating)

(A) Simple random sample

(B) Convenience sample

(C) Stratified random sample

(D) Judgment sample

2. The WLP professional works with two sales groups on a project to measure knowledge acquisition on new product enhancements. The first group is tested and receives formal training. The second group is tested and does not receive training. After two weeks both group are retested. What is the second group called? (Measuring and Evaluating)

(A) Experimental group

(B) Pre-measured group

(C) Control group

(D) Sample group

3. The management at a restaurant notices a steady decline in the servers' performance levels. The management hires a consultant to investigate this issue and find a possible solution. The consultant concludes that the servers lack a clear understanding of the desired performance requirements. To improve performance, the consultant would most likely suggest setting up: (Improving Human Performance)

(A) a feedback system

(B) performance standards

(C) a performance system

(D) performance training

4. Which of the following is used to determine the specific functions of a position? (Career Planning and Talent Management)

(A) Needs assessment

(B) Skills hierarchies

(C) Gap analysis

(D) Job analysis

5. Which of the following are relevant output units identified for performance at the organizational, process, and/or individual levels? (Improving Human Performance)

(A) Capacity motivation units

(B) Process intervention metrics

(C) Performance measures

(D) Goal performance events

6. A reaction (Level 1) evaluation is used to: (Delivering Training)

(A) identify the needs and prior knowledge of students

(B) make a judgment about the level of achievement of a student

(C) determine the satisfaction level with a learning experience

(D) assist with gap analysis

7. Which of the following is a component of a task assessment? (Career Planning and Talent Management)

(A) Conditions under which the tasks are performed

(B) Review of the effectiveness of the job incumbents

(C) A list of all of the competencies of the job

(D) An inventory of employee attitudes

8. The principle of over-learning is best defined by which of the following? (Designing Learning)

(A) Practice beyond the point where performance is consistently demonstrated

(B) Learning of discrete task parts that make up the complete task in spaced practice

(C) A combination of massed and spaced practice

(D) A series of mental or cognitive rehearsals using a massed approach to learning

9. Which of the following is a good method for presenting information to learners who have an auditory learning preference? (Delivering Training)

(A) Glossaries

(B) Field trips

(C) Pictures

(D) Discussions

10. Appreciative inquiry is an approach to analysis that is helpful to a WLP professional interested in identifying which of the following? (Facilitating Organizational Change)

(A) Reasons for resistance to change

(B) The positive elements to carry forward

(C) Ways of building and maintaining trust

(D) Problems and difficulties to resolve

Answer Key

1. A
2. C
3. B
4. D
5. C
6. C
7. A
8. A
9. D
10. B

4
The Work Product

After you earn a passing score on the knowledge-based exam, it is time to finalize your Work Product for submission—Part II, or Exam II, of the certification process. The Work Product portion of the certification process requires that you submit a project you have completed in the past three years. The project should be a sample or a segment of your past work and not an entire portfolio or body of work.

The ASTD CI estimates that it will take you approximately 60 hours to prepare your submission. You should allow additional time to obtain the necessary signatures for the Work Product Release Document, which contains participant release signatures. Once you receive notification that you passed the knowledge-based exam, you will have approximately eight to 12 weeks to submit your Work Product, so plan carefully.

Because the Work Product will be a blind submission, it is important that you provide sufficient evidence and carefully address the program requirements. In other words, the rating teams that evaluate your submission will not have any information about you, such as the number of years of experience you have or the quality of other work you have completed. Thus, it is very important that you pick the right AOE and the right segment of your project to submit.

But which AOE should you choose? What are the guidelines? It is important to refer to the Candidate Bulletin online at www.astd.org/astd/cplp for the most current information and specific guidelines about Work Product submissions. For now, let's turn to a discussion of the requirements. First, we'll focus on what each Work Product has in common. Then, we will focus on what's unique by AOE.

Work Product Forms and Materials

Your completed Work Product application must contain the following additional forms or materials. See Appendix D, Work Product Timeline, for more information about submitting these materials.

- **Identification and Contact Information**, which includes your identifying information (name, ASTD CI Customer number, Candidate ID number, and contact information)

- **Work Product Release Document**, which confirms that the materials you submit are your own work and grants ASTD CI permission to evaluate the materials you submit; it also provides release documentation for the collaborators on the learning design project. More than one copy of this form may be submitted

- **Work Product Submission Form** (i.e., summary description of your Work Product and text identifying location of core components—project relationships, Plans, outputs, outcomes—within the Work Product)

- **Work Product Supporting Evidence** (your answers to the eight provided questions)

- **Follow-On Question 1** and **Follow-On Question 2** which will be mailed to you following the close of the knowledge-based exam window

- **Your Knowledge Test Passing Score Report**.

Scoring

Scoring committee members will evaluate your respective Designing Learning, Delivering Training, or Measuring and Evaluating Work Product based on your summary description, the evidence of the key elements in your Work Product, and your responses to the supporting evidence questions.

You will be evaluated on these four core components:

Project relationships: This section describes how the project relates to your stakeholders.

Plans: This section documents your efforts in planning the Work Product. Be sure to identify your organization's needs and requirements. Here, you'll collect and analyze any relevant data and present your design solutions.

Outputs: This section documents Work Product outputs such as implementing solutions and managing resources.

Outcomes: This section documents your results during and after the implementation of the Work Product (for example, evaluating results and monitoring progress).

Work Product submissions are broken out into the four key areas, regardless of AOE. Six scores generated:

- one score for *each* of the four core components as it relates to your Work Product (this includes answers to the Supporting Evidence questions)

- one score for your response to follow-on question 1

- one score for your response to follow-on question 2.

The maximum possible score is 18 points. You can score up to three points in each area as follows:

3 = Outstanding

2 = Successful

1 = Limited Success

0 = Blank or Off Topic

Subject matter experts in the Designing Learning, Delivering Training, and Measuring and Evaluating AOEs will serve as scorers. Candidate submissions will be presented to scorers in random order. Each submission will be scored twice. If scorers' results are more than one point apart or if there are two scores of 0, the submission will be adjudicated. Tables 4-1 and 4-2 show examples of approved score results and score results that will require adjudication.

Table 4-1. Approved Score Results

Category	Score 1	Score 2	Requiring Adjudication?
Project Relationships	3	3	No
Plans	2	3	No
Output	3	3	No
Outcomes	0	1	No
Follow-On Question 1	2	1	No
Follow-On Question 2	3	2	No

Table 4-2. Score Results Requiring Adjudication

Category	Score 1	Score 2	Requiring Adjudication?
Project Relationships	3	1	Yes
Plans	3	3	No
Output	3	2	No
Outcomes	3	3	No
Follow-On Question 1	1	3	Yes
Follow-On Question 2	0	0	Yes

The maximum possible score is 18. The passing score is 12. A compensatory model will be used, meaning it will not be necessary to obtain a minimum score in any one category. A score of 0 will result in a failing score regardless of the total.

Tip: You may be very familiar with the Work Product you submit, but the scorers reviewing your submission are not. They will have a short time to clearly understand the nature of your project and identify your level of competency from the materials you submit. Be clear, concise, and thorough when compiling your submission. Be sure to follow the Work Product submission guidelines carefully.

Work Product Supporting Evidence

Your scores in the four core components are derived from a combination of sources. Not only will raters be looking at your actual Work Product but also at your responses to questions about your submission. This combination gives the rater a fuller picture of your submission. The description and the answers provide additional information about the content and the processes that are evidenced in your Work Product.

Follow-On Questions

In addition to the core components described above, you will be presented with two follow-on questions; essay responses will be required for each.

Tip: The follow-on questions are just as important as your Work Product. Be sure to give clear and thoughtful answers that thoroughly address each follow-on question.

The purpose of the follow-on questions is to demonstrate application of knowledge in a different setting or circumstances than found in your Work Product. The first part of the response to the follow-on question is a summary description of the project that you provided on the Work Product Submission Form. This summary is to provide scorers with a context for your answer to the follow-on question, who will not have access to your Work Product during the scoring session. Although you may wish to refer to your Work Product as examples when you respond to the question, the most successful response will address each of the points or issues described in the question, providing evidence of how the issue might be addressed.

Work Product by AOE

Now let's look at some of the specific AOE guidelines of the Work Product submission. The following sections merely present an overview of the requirements by AOE—keep in mind that it is very important to review the detailed guidelines at www.astd.org/astd/cplp prior to compiling your Work Product.

ASTD CI recognizes that submission of a Work Product includes providing information that may be proprietary to a company. ASTD staff involvement is bound by contract disclosure.

Tip: If you don't have the deliverables described for any of the designated AOEs, ASTD CI will discuss requirements with individuals on a case-by-case basis. Contact certification@astd.org.

Designing Learning

If you select to submit a Designing Learning Work Product, you must provide the following three documents:

- training analysis documentation
- design document
- curriculum or representative material for a 90-minute segment of learning

The foundation of the Designing Learning Work Product is the 11 key actions (KA) from the *ASTD Competency Study: Mapping the Future* (ASTD, 2004):

KA 1. Applies cognition and adult learning theory
KA 2. Collaborates with others
KA 3. Conducts a needs assessment

KA 4. Designs a curriculum or program
KA 5. Creates designs or specifications for instructional material
KA 6. Analyzes and selects technologies
KA 7. Integrates technology options
KA 8. Develops instructional materials
KA 9. Evaluates learning design
KA 10. Manages others
KA 11. Manages and implements projects.

Training Analysis Documentation

The ASTD CI recognizes that designing learning can result in an online course, a classroom session, a self-paced workbook, and many other learning events.

You should include evidence of the following categories in your training analysis documentation:

- data collection methodology

- data analysis

- recommendations

- conclusions.

Table 4-3 provides suggestions of appropriate items for the training analysis documentation. These are suggestions only. The specific documentation will depend on the objectives of the learning event. You will need to select the documentation you have for your Work Product that addresses the categories of evidence.

Table 4-3. Suggested Documentation Items

Category	Suggested Items
Data collection methodology	<ul><li>assessment instrument(s) or tool(s)</li><li>summary of how data was collected (focus groups, interviews, surveys, etc.)</li><li>summary of who data was collected from</li><li>summary of why collection methods were selected</li></ul>
Data analysis	Summary of the data analysis for<ul><li>business need</li><li>learning need</li><li>performance requirements</li><li>learning environment</li><li>audience profile</li><li>job or task affected</li></ul>

Category	Suggested Items
Recommendations	• ways to adapt or modify the learning approaches to the target audience based on the data from the training analysis • link of learning solution to strategic business objectives
Conclusions	• comparison of the solution/intervention options considered • cost-benefit analysis of various solution/intervention options • risk analysis (constraints and issues) of various solution/intervention options

Design Document

At a minimum, your design document must contain the following:

- project overview
- development timeline
- learning/performance objectives
- plan for evaluation
- topical outline
- identification of source content
- chosen delivery medium(s)
- description of learning activities.

Curriculum or Learning Materials

The documents you provide as a representation of the curriculum or materials for the learning activities will depend on the objectives and, in most cases, delivery mode selected. Table 4-4 lists the types of documents that you can submit as evidence of development.

Table 4-4. Suggested Curriculum Documents

Delivery Mode	Example Outputs
Classroom training	• lesson plans • trainer's guide • handouts • learner's workbook • overheads • supply list
On-the-job training	• task checklist • handouts • job aids • learner's workbook • material/supply list
Self-instruction	• learner's workbook • content for a CD-ROM for computer-based modules* • list of reference materials • storyboard for video • script for audio
Web-based training	• content for a CD-ROM* • storyboards • scripts

Note: Do not submit the CD-ROM. Hardcopy content is required.

The raters will be looking for certain key elements when they review your actual Work Product (your project work). The key elements are based on the key actions from the ASTD Competency Model, but are often more specific. The following are the key elements the raters will be looking for in your actual Work Product (your project work):

Project Relationships:

- Defined goals, roles, and responsibilities of the project.
- Communicated with stakeholders through the pilot phase of the project

Planning:

- Collected and analyzed data.
- Compared options and made recommendations and/or decisions based on data analysis.
- Designed curriculum to meet needs identified.

Outputs:

- Wrote measurable learning/performance objectives.

- Developed content that was logically linked and sequenced.

- Designed, developed, and evaluated learning activities and learning materials.

- Included opportunities for practice, enrichment, and assessment.

Outcomes:

- Designed and developed assessment activities that will (would) show achievement of the learning objectives.

- Developed summative and/or formative evaluation plan.

Designing Learning Supporting Evidence

Your Work Product submission documentation will also include the answers to several questions designed to provide a complete picture of your project. For example, a question might ask: "Describe the adult learning theory and principles you used to design the curriculum or learning materials." If you describe addressing the visual-auditory-kinesthetic model, then the curriculum should contain a variety of materials that address all three types of learners. If you state that the training analysis identified the need for a job aid, then the training analysis documentation should include the data that supports this conclusion and a job aid should be included in the learning materials portion of the submission. The design document should have learning objectives that support adult learning and the resulting course or learning materials should have activities or materials that match the learning objectives. How the learning theory was applied should be evident throughout the Work Product. You can view these questions on the ASTD CI website Candidate Bulletin for Designing Learning.

Designing Learning Follow-On Example

Below is a sample of a follow-on question for the Designing Learning AOE and an analysis of the points that a successful response would address.

Question: Your project was designed for an organization. A merger between that organization and a multinational organization has occurred. You are asked to redesign the project to meet the needs of these newly merged employees, while creating a new corporate culture from the two organizations. Describe what you will do and how you will do it.

- This sample follow-on question includes four different key points:

- The need to redesign the Work Product is the result of a merger.

- The new organization will have multinational needs.

- The employee needs must be addressed.

- A new corporate culture will emerge.

Analysis: A complete answer will provide a description of what is to be done and how it will be accomplished from each of the four perspectives.

Delivering Training

If you select to submit a Delivering Training Work Product, you will submit a recording of a learning session in which you demonstrate the competencies associated with delivering and facilitating learning.

The foundation of the delivering training Work Product is the 12 key actions (KA) from the *ASTD Competency Study: Mapping the Future* (ASTD, 2004):

KA 1. Prepares for training delivery

KA 2. Aligns learning solutions with course objectives and learner needs

KA 3. Conveys objectives

KA 4. Delivers various learning methodologies

KA 5. Facilitates learning

KA 6. Encourages participation and builds learner motivation

KA 7. Establishes credibility as instructor

KA 8. Manages the learning environment

KA 9.   Delivers constructive feedback

KA 10. Creates a positive learning climate

KA 11. Ensures learning outcomes

KA 12. Evaluates solutions

You are required to provide the following:

- a videotape or CD of a 20-minute instructor-led class session or synchronous e-learning session
- a facilitator's guide for the session on the video or CD.

A learning session is a short module within a longer learning event. One learning activity cannot serve as the entire learning session. The learning session must be synchronous and instructor-led and must involve six or more learners. The learning session may take place in a classroom or in a web-based setting. The recorded learning session must provide clear, observable evidence of the interaction between the instructor and the learners, and the learners must be observable at least at the beginning of the recording.

Selecting an appropriate segment to submit is an important element of a successful recording. For example, the first 20 minutes of a course in which the learners introduce themselves for 15 minutes would not provide the necessary evidence that the learners have learned. Although trainer presentation skills are important elements of a successful session, they should not be the only competency demonstrated.

Tip: Scorers are not just evaluating your ability to lecture or your presentation skills. They are also interested in how well you facilitate learning and the interaction you have with your learners.

The raters will be looking for certain key elements when they review your actual Work Product (your recording). The key elements are based on the key actions from the ASTD Competency Model, but are often more specific. The following are the key elements the raters will be looking for in your actual Work Product (your recording):

Project relationships:

- Created a positive learning climate

- Defined goals, roles and responsibilities of the project

Planning:

- Conveyed objectives.

- Linked objectives to on-the-job performance.

- Managed the learning environment.

Outputs:

- Aligned learning solutions with course objectives and learner needs.

- Delivered various learning methodologies.

- Facilitated learning.

- Encouraged participation and built learner motivation.

- Established credibility as an instructor.

- Delivered constructive feedback.

Outcomes:

- Aligned learning solutions with course objectives and learner needs.

- Monitored learner progress in learning acquisition.

- Ensured learning outcomes.

Delivering Training Supporting Evidence

Again, your scores in the four core components are derived from a combination of sources. Not only will raters be looking at your actual Work Product (your recording), but also at your responses to questions about your submission. This combination gives the rater a fuller picture of your submission.

For example, a question might ask, "Describe the planning steps you took to address the logistics for the learning environment, the materials, and the media used in the training activity." If your description includes that you prepared handouts, then the handouts should be observable on the video. If a hands-on activity is planned to support the kinesthetic learner, at least some part of that activity should be included in the video. The room setup in the video should match what is described. If it is an e-learning session in which the plan calls for a "virtual whiteboard exercise", then that exercise should be recorded, at least in part. It is the combination of the responses and the video that will result in the score for planning.

Delivering Training Follow-On Example

Below is a sample follow-on question for the Delivering Training AOE and an analysis of the points that a successful response would address.

Question: During one of the times you deliver this learning session, you ask learners to complete one of the activities. They object and want to use the time to work on something else that is outside the scope of the learning objectives. Describe how you would accommodate the learners' request and yet meet the learning objectives within the allowable time.

- This sample follow-on question includes four different key points:
- The learners object, but no reason has been stated why.
- The learners are interested in something outside the scope of the event.
- The learning environment may influence how the accommodation may be made.
- The learning objectives must be met.

Analysis: A complete answer will address those elements, including recognition of the characteristics of the learners and the internal and the external environment that may influence the actions taken.

Measuring and Evaluating

If you select the Measuring and Evaluating AOE, the foundation of your Work Product is the six key actions (KA) from the *ASTD Competency Study: Mapping the Future* (ASTD, 2004):

KA 1. Identifies customer expectations

KA 2. Selects or designs appropriate strategies, research design, and measures

KA 3. Communicates and gains support for the measurement and evaluation plan

KA 4. Manages data collection

KA 5. Analyzes and interprets data

KA 6. Reports conclusions and makes recommendations based on findings.

The Measuring and Evaluating Work Product is a report of an actual evaluation of a learning activity. The evaluation report must fully describe the evaluation project conducted.

A complete evaluation report often contains the following components. The evidence for each of the major elements should be provided through components such as described in Table 4-5.

Table 4-5. Evaluation Report

Section	Report Item
Title	• Provide the title of the program or project that was evaluated
Dates	• Provide the following dates: (1) the date when the program or project was conducted, (2) the date when the evaluation was conducted, and (3) the date when the report was prepared.
Methodology or strategy	• Provide a full description of the methodology or the strategy that was employed for the evaluation. This might include: • evaluation objectives • level(s) of evaluation measured (you may use either the Kirkpatrick four-level or the Phillips five-level method) • stakeholder involvement • experimental design and rationale (including a description of the sample size) • data collection tool(s) used (attachments of example tools would be referenced here) and how they were administered • description of the business metrics collected and how they were collected if business impact data were used, or the formula and the cost data that were used if an

Section	Report Item
	return-on-investment (ROI) analysis or benefit-cost (BCR) analysis was conducted • timelines for the data collection, analysis, and reporting • discussion of the analysis conducted on the data, including statistical tests run and the rationale for using the tests • method for isolating the impact of the program if measured for performance or organizational impact • method to convert benefits to monetary value if measured for ROI or BCR • method used to prepare the results for communication to stakeholders.
Results	Provide the results of the analysis, including tables, charts, or graphs that summarize and present the results in an easy-to-understand manner. Detailed data or raw data can be referenced as an appendix. Important items to include are • summarized (quantified) data • response rate • areas of significance • results of calculations • significant comments, intangible benefits, or other qualified data.
Conclusions	State the conclusions for the project that you have derived from the results.
Recommendations (optional)	If you offered recommendations based on the conclusions, list them in this section.
Communication	Discuss the way in which the evaluation results were communicated, to whom, and in what manner. Provide reactions to the presentations, if any.
Appendixes	You may or may not have appendices in your report, depending on the evaluation design. Appendixes could include: • data collection or ROI analysis plans • questionnaires or surveys used • interview reports • measurement tools used • data summary tables

Section	Report Item
	• tables of data from individual regions or groups if they were combined in the body of the report
	• results of previous relevant studies.

Although the description above is used to provide general guidance about the Measuring and Evaluating Work Product, it is not meant to be prescriptive. The focus of your Work Product is to provide evidence that demonstrates the key actions outlined above.

In addition, you are expected to provide a summary description of your Work Product (Work Product Submission Form) and answers to the questions (Work Product Supporting Evidence). The key elements are based on the key actions from the ASTD Competency Model that we described earlier, but are often more specific. The following are the key elements the raters will be looking for in your actual Work Product (your project work):

Project Relationships:

- participants of the program
- audience for the evaluation report
- people who provided data for the evaluation

Planning:

- description of business goals and program objectives
- description of data collection plan
- description of data analysis plan

Output:

- instruments (surveys, tests, protocols, checklists, etc.)
- description of data and sample
- quantitative results
- qualitative results

Outcomes:

- conclusions
- recommendations

Measuring and Evaluating Supporting Evidence

Again, your scores in the four core components are derived from a combination of sources. Not only will raters be looking at your actual Work Product (your project work) but also at your responses to questions about your submission. This combination gives the rater a fuller picture of your submission.

Following is an example of the interplay that should exist between your Work Product (your project) and the questions. For example, if a question asks, "Describe how you balanced the need for technical accuracy with practical organizational considerations and/or other constraints." If you describe challenges with obtaining the appropriate sample, your report should include explanations for sample size or computations to compensate for a low sample size. Your report should include an analysis of qualitative data if you respond that you used it in lieu of quantitative data as part of the research.

However you describe the tradeoffs that influenced your research, the evidence of how you actually accommodated those tradeoffs should be easily identifiable in the report. It is the combination of the responses and the report that will result in the score for planning.

Measuring and Evaluating Follow-On Example

Below is a sample follow-on question for the Measuring and Evaluating AOE and an analysis of the points that a successful response would address.

Question: Management has reviewed your report and is so impressed that they want you to do this for every project going forward. What would be your response?

Four different key points are included in this follow-on sample:

- Management interest requires consideration of management perspective.
- Every project might not fit the process used for your particular project.
- Management is impressed, so it might not be a good idea to challenge the request.
- What parts of the methodology will stay the same and what parts will need to change will depend on the circumstances.

Analysis: A complete answer will address those elements, including recognition of what management is likely to care about that may require a change in emphasis such as the impact on strategy or the bottom line.

Pitfalls

See Appendix C, "Common Pitfalls," for a list of common pitfalls and guidance on how to avoid them.

For more information about preparing your Work Product submissions, please refer to the Candidate Bulletin at www.astd.org/astd/cplp/cand_bul.htm. The Candidate Bulletin will provide

- descriptions of the forms and materials required for the application packet
- general directions for the Work Product application
- a description of the Work Product scoring process
- a sample of the Work Product Scoring Committee nondisclosure agreement
- AOE-specific directions for the Work Product application
- samples of the forms required for a complete application packet
- scoring guidelines for the Work Product submissions.

5
The *ASTD Learning System*

Let's take a look inside the *ASTD Learning System*. These examples will illustrate just some of what the modules contain.

Chapter Introductions

Every chapter begins with an introduction and a list of learning objectives. Below is a typical example of a chapter introduction and list of learning objectives from Module 2: *Delivering Training*, Chapter 4, "Training Delivery Options and Media":

4
Training Delivery Options and Media

Regardless of the setting, adult educators must recognize the many different avenues of delivery. Each avenue has inherent characteristics as well as different learner demographics and motivations that all WLP professionals should be comfortable with. It's valuable for WLP professionals to understand all the different delivery options so that they have some control over the presentation. The facilitator also should be able to provide insight and make recommendations regarding the delivery of the content.

A WLP professional should be comfortable with all delivery options. E-learning promotes self-directedness, and busy professionals are pleased to have this option. Web-based learning should be applicable to all learning settings, regardless of the environment; the same should also be true of classroom, blended, and multimedia delivery. As a starting point, facilitators should be able to identify the characteristics, value, and applicability of each option and have a thorough knowledge of delivery terminology.

Chapter heading, or key knowledge area. Note: Pay attention to the introductions! They often contain valuable information.

Learning Objectives:

- ☑ Define environmental considerations that ensure optimal classroom learning.
- ☑ Discuss the benefits of message boards and chat rooms to learning groups and online communities.
- ☑ State two benefits of web-based training (WBT) and list two requirements with regard to audio and video plug-ins.
- ☑ Discuss two examples of when classroom learning or e-learning are most appropriately used and explain why.
- ☑ Define blended learning.
- ☑ State the purpose of an electronic performance support system (EPSS) and discuss when to use or not use an EPSS.

Learning objectives focus content.

Sample Page

Below is a sample page from Module 1: *Designing Learning*. Throughout the text, you will see key terms italicized in bold. These terms can also be found in the glossary, or Appendix A of the module.

Abraham Maslow's Hierarchy of Needs

Motivating people to achieve their potential is one of the challenges in learning and performance improvement. To explain the foundations of motivation, Abraham Maslow introduced his hierarchy of needs in *Motivation and Personality*, published in 1954. Maslow contended that people have complex needs that they strive to fulfill and that over time, their needs change and evolve.

Maslow (1954) categorized these needs into a logical hierarchy from physical to psychological (illustrated in Figure 1-1):

- ***Physiological***: These needs include food, drink, sex, and sleep.
- ***Safety***: These include freedom from fear and the need to be safe and stable.
- ***Belongingness***: This category concerns the need for friends and family.
- ***Esteem***: This includes both self-esteem and the need to be highly regarded by others.
- ***Self-actualization***: This is the need to be "all that you can be."

Figure 1-1. Maslow's Hierarchy of Needs

Source: Sharpe (1991).

Maslow contended that a person can achieve the next higher level of the hierarchy only after lower-level needs have been satisfied. This means that employees and learners are motivated by a variety of factors—and that those factors may be unknown or difficult to discern.

Most jobs satisfy needs in the four lower levels of the hierarchy: wages or salaries to provide for physiological needs, a safe working environment, camaraderie for belongingness needs, and the respect of co-workers and peers for esteem. Needs related to self-actualization link to the number and types of opportunities for growth and achievement the work provides. For WLP professionals, understanding learner motivation and factors influencing motivation is one piece of the designing learning puzzle. Establishing an appropriate climate and a sense of safety in a learning environment will help to satisfy the lower-level needs of adult learners.

Malcolm Knowles's Adult Learning, or Andragogy

Malcolm Knowles, a leader in the field of adult education, was one of the first researchers to propose that adults learn differently than children. In his seminal book,

---

Key terms are explained.

Figures and tables show models, charts, and processes.

Section headings and content are drawn from content outline points.

Knowledge Checks

Every chapter (with the exception of Crossover chapters) of the *ASTD Learning System* contains a ***Knowledge Check*** section consisting of true-or-false and multiple-choice questions to help you study. These questions' format is similar to that found on the exam. Here is an example of a Knowledge Check from Module 4: *Measuring and Evaluating*:

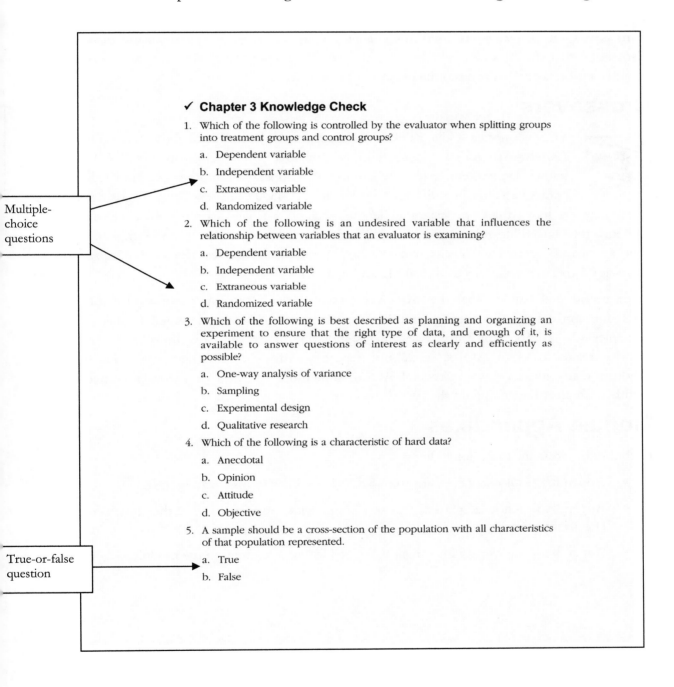

Multiple-choice questions

True-or-false question

✓ **Chapter 3 Knowledge Check**

1. Which of the following is controlled by the evaluator when splitting groups into treatment groups and control groups?

   a. Dependent variable

   b. Independent variable

   c. Extraneous variable

   d. Randomized variable

2. Which of the following is an undesired variable that influences the relationship between variables that an evaluator is examining?

   a. Dependent variable

   b. Independent variable

   c. Extraneous variable

   d. Randomized variable

3. Which of the following is best described as planning and organizing an experiment to ensure that the right type of data, and enough of it, is available to answer questions of interest as clearly and efficiently as possible?

   a. One-way analysis of variance

   b. Sampling

   c. Experimental design

   d. Qualitative research

4. Which of the following is a characteristic of hard data?

   a. Anecdotal

   b. Opinion

   c. Attitude

   d. Objective

5. A sample should be a cross-section of the population with all characteristics of that population represented.

   a. True

   b. False

Terminology

The *ASTD Learning System* uses language that should be familiar to the practicing WLP professional. Each module contains a glossary (Appendix A) with terms relevant to its particular AOE. In addition, as you read through the chapters, you will find key terms in bold italic.

In general, the term WLP professional is used to refer to professionals in the field. The terms *learner* and *participant* are used interchangeably, as are the terms *facilitator* and *trainer*. Also note that in Module 7: *Coaching* the terms *employee* and *client* are often used interchangeably when referring to the person being coached.

Crossovers

You will notice a chain link icon (shown at left) used throughout the *ASTD Learning System*. This icon, called a **crossover**, will help you "link" a key knowledge content chapter where the icon appears to another key knowledge content chapter in a different module in the *ASTD Learning System*. Crossovers are usually no more than two pages in length, include a single learning objective, and reference the "linked" learning system module and knowledge area. Here is an example of a typical crossover reference: "To learn more about these principles, see Module 1, *Designing Learning*, Chapter 1, 'Cognition and Adult Learning Theory.'"

There are several reasons that the crossover sections exist. Primarily, there are theories, ideas, and applications that span several AOEs (for example, Measurement and Evaluation principles). It is important from a learning standpoint to explain how those ideas and theories relate to other AOEs, while not repeating information unnecessarily. Lastly, although many ideas crossover several AOEs, sometimes the idea or theory is applied slightly differently depending on the AOE.

Module Appendixes

Each module contains three appendixes:

- Appendix A: Glossary contains the bold, italicized key terms from the text.
- Appendix B: Knowledge Check answer key provides answers to all of the knowledge checks, by chapter.
- Appendix C: Index provides an alphabetized listing of content in the module.

In addition, Module 4, *Measuring and Evaluating*, Module 8, *Managing Organizational Change*, and Module 7, *Coaching*, each contain an Appendix D: Case Studies. These are real-world case studies pulled from ASTD Press *In Action* series books. Module 7 also contains Appendix E—the entire bibliography of references for the *ASTD Learning System*.

6
Test Preparation

No matter the study method you choose, we suggest you follow this three-step process:

Step 1: Study, Study, Study

Thoroughly review the content presented in the *ASTD Learning System* and any other reference materials you choose. Be sure to pay special attention to the Knowledge Check questions at the end of each chapter, which will ensure that you are thinking along the appropriate lines.

You should give yourself at least six to eight weeks to fully prepare for the exam. If you work full time and need to review all nine AOEs, a realistic time frame would be two weeks for each AOE—or 20 hours each. Please note that we cannot guarantee success on the exam.

Step 2: Identify Strengths, Weaknesses

Answer the knowledge check questions to calibrate the level of difficulty of the test questions. Use the questions to determine areas in which you excel and areas you need to reinforce. Remember: Don't limit your review to your areas of weakness—you need to sharpen all of your skills.

Step 3: Review, Review, Review

Check out the knowledge check questions again and make sure you are familiar with the material *and* the exam format.

Once you've completed your course of study and have sufficiently prepared for the exam, sit back and relax. Avoid the temptation to conduct a late-night cram session the night before the exam. Remember, this exam tests a broad overview of material, not minute details. Obscure names and dates of events will not be part of the test.

Preparation Methods

There are myriad ways to prepare for the exam. The method you choose will depend on your time, budget, and learning preferences. Some suggestions include

- *self-study*: study alone using a library of up-to-date learning resources
- *study buddy*: pair up with members who have different strengths by sharing your knowledge; you will broaden your area of expertise
- *group study*: join a study group to help divide the labor and build esprit de corps.

If you choose to establish an official study group, remember to appoint a coordinator for the study program. Coordinators usually

- counsel professionals who are debating whether to take the exam

- publicize the certification through articles and flyers

- act as a liaison with ASTD CI on certification issues

- coordinate the application process

- acknowledge newly certified members.

The following are some additional general preparation and confidence building tips, adapted from "Study Guides and Strategies" (2005).

Review Your Personal Situation and Skills

- Develop good study habits and strategies.

- Manage time (dealing with procrastination, distractions, laziness).

- Organizing material to be studied and learned.

- Take a step-by-step approach to build a strategy and not get overwhelmed.

- Avoid outside pressures: success/failure consequences, peer pressure, or competitiveness, and so forth.

- Review your past performance on tests to improve and learn from the experience.

Test Preparation to Reduce Anxiety

- Approach the exam with confidence; use whatever strategies you can to personalize success: visualization, logic, talking to yourself, practice, team work, journaling, and so forth. View the exam as an opportunity to show how much you have studied and to receive a reward for the studying you have done.

- Be prepared! Learn your material thoroughly and organize the materials you will need for the test. Use a checklist.

- Allow yourself plenty of time, especially to do things you need to do before the test and still get there a little early.

- Avoid thinking you need to cram just before the test.

- Strive for a relaxed state of concentration. Avoid speaking with any fellow exam takers who have not prepared, who express negativity, who will distract your preparation.

- Sharpen the mind with a good exercise program.

- Get a good night's sleep the night before the exam.

- Don't go to the exam on an empty stomach. Fresh fruits and vegetables are often recommended to reduce stress. Avoid stress-producing foods, such as processed foods, artificial sweeteners, carbonated soft drinks, chocolate, eggs, fried foods, junk foods, pork, red meat, sugar, white flour products, chips and similar snack foods, and foods containing preservatives or heavy spices.

You are now on your way to becoming a Certified Professional in Learning and Performance! No matter which study method or methods you choose, we hope that you will find the *ASTD Learning System* to be a valuable tool in preparing for the exam portion of the certification process.

References

Bernthal, P.R., et al. (2004). *ASTD 2004 Competency Study: Mapping the Future*. Alexandria, VA: ASTD Press.

Naughton, J.N. (2005). CPLP Candidate Bulletin. Available at http://www.astd.org/astd/cplp. Alexandria, VA: ASTD CI.

Russo, C.S., editor. (2005). *Early Bird Guide to ASTD Professional Certification*. Alexandria, VA: ASTD Press. (out of print)

"Study Guides and Strategies." (2005). Available at http://www.studygs.net/index.htm.

Appendix A
AOE Module Contents

Module 1: Designing Learning

1. **Cognition and Adult Learning Theory**

   The Role of Adult Learning Theories in Designing Instruction
   Four Theories of Learning and Instruction
   Abraham Maslow's Hierarchy of Needs
   Malcolm Knowles's Adult Learning, or Andragogy
   Adult Development Theories
   Three Types of Learning and Bloom's Taxonomy
   Differences Between Teaching and Facilitating Learning
   Guidelines for Facilitating Learning
   Individual Characteristics of Learning
   Theories of Learning and Memory
   The Learning Brain Model
   Neurolinguistic Programming and Modes of Learning
   External and Environmental Influences
   Multiple Intelligences

2. **Instructional Design Theory and Process**

   Principles Guiding Training Design
   Theories and Models for Designing Instruction
   Basics of Course Design
   Basics of Course Development

3. **An Exploration of Instructional Methods**

   Instructional Strategies
   Active Training Techniques
   E-Learning Techniques

4. **Various Delivery Options and Media**

5. **Job and Task Analysis and Competency Modeling**

6. **Content Knowledge and Content From SMEs**

   Collaboration With SMEs to Identify Instructional Needs

7. **Assessment Methods and Formats**

   The Purpose of Needs Assessment
   Steps to Conduct a Needs Assessment
   Levels of Needs Assessment
   Data-Collection Methods
   Results of Needs Assessment

8. **Learning Technologies and Support Systems**

9. **New and Emerging Learning Technologies and Support Systems**

10. **Business Strategy, Drivers, or Needs Associated With Learning Interventions**

11. **Research Methods**

12. **Individual, Group, and Organizational Differences That Influence Learning**

13. **Legal and Ethical Issues Related to Designing Learning**

14. **Differences Between E-Learning and Traditional Courses**

    Comparison of Classroom Training and E-Learning
    Advantages of E-Learning
    Disadvantages of E-Learning
    Advantages of Classroom Learning
    Disadvantages of Classroom Learning
    Blended Learning
    E-Learning Implementation and Evaluation Considerations

15. **Design of Information Displays, Access, and Resources**

Module 2: Delivering Training

1. **Adult Learning Theories and Techniques**

2. **Instructional Design Theory and Methods**

3. **Instructional Methods**

4. **Training Delivery Options and Media**

   Classroom Training
   E-Learning
   When to Use E-Learning or Classroom Training
   Blended Learning
   Performance Support Systems
   Self-Study

5. **Existing Learning Technologies and Support Systems**

6. **Emerging Learning Technologies and Support Systems**

7. **Presentation Techniques and Tools**

   Creating a Learning Climate

   Preparing for Training Delivery

   Understanding Basic Classroom Management

   Using Icebreakers, Opening Exercises, and Closing Activities

   Understanding Presentation Behavior

   Facilitating Learning Activities

   Performing on-the-Spot Assessment of Participants' Success in Achieving Program
     Objectives

   Understanding the Differences Between Delivering Live Training Online and Classroom
     Training

   Devising Strategies for Keeping Participants Interested and Involved

   Using Presentation and Training Tools

8. **Organizational Work Environment and Systems**

9. **Individual Learning Styles**

   Theories of How Humans Learn Best

   Herrmann's Brain-Based Approach to Learning

   Neurolinguistic Programming and Modes of Learning

   Accelerated Learning Techniques

   Learning Style Inventories

   Factors Affecting the Speed at Which Adults Learn

   Importance of Identifying Training and Presenting Styles

   Awareness of Matching Learner and Trainer Styles

   Tools for Determining Learning Preferences

   Importance of Training Needs Assessment

10. **Cultural Differences**

    Barriers to Communication

    Culture Concepts

    Impact of Culture on Learning Styles Training

    Emerging Issues in Adult Education

11. **Familiarity With Content Being Taught and How the Solution Addresses the
    Need**

    The Importance of Preparing Content

12. **Legal and Ethical Issues Relevant for Delivering Training**

Module 3: Improving Human Performance

1. **Human Performance Improvement**

   Purpose and Goals of HPI
   Differences Between HPI and Training
   Factors That Affect Human Performance
   Human Performance Models
   Integration of HPI Parts
   Differences Between Improving Performance Versus Providing Specific Solutions
   Relationship Between the Big-Picture Goals of an Organization and the Initiative
   Role of Strong Change Management

2. **Business, Performance, and Gap Analysis**

   Business Analysis
   External Analysis
   Performance Analysis
   Project Scope
   Measurement Criteria and Desired Performance Outcomes
   Constraints Analysis
   Cultural Analysis
   Gap Analysis
   Workflow Analysis
   Analysis Tools
   Human Resource Needs Forecasting

3. **Root Cause Analysis**

   Root Causes
   Tools for Root Cause Analysis
   Importance of Gathering Data

4. **Intervention Selection and Implementation**

   Intervention Selection Overview
   Population Analysis
   Resource Analysis
   Potential Solutions
   Improving Structure and Process
   Improving Resources
   Improving Information
   Improving Knowledge and Skills
   Improving Motives
   Improving Wellness

Decision-Making Matrixes and Methods
Common Mistakes
Change Management
Budgeting and Cost
Importance of Describing Solutions
Ethics and Integrity
Networking

5. **Measurement and Evaluation**

6. **Change Management**

7. **HPI Models**

ASTD HPI Model
Alternate Models

8. **Systems Thinking and Theory**

Systems Thinking
Cultural and Global Awareness
Mergers and Acquisitions Management
Industry Knowledge
Broad Company Knowledge
System Archetypes

9. **Group Dynamics Process**

Issues Associated With Group Dynamics
Tuckman Model
Cog's Ladder

10. **Facilitation Methods**

Facilitation and Team Development
Questioning Techniques
Meeting Management
Process Mapping
Process Improvement Methodologies
Decision-Making Methods and Processes
Group Dynamics, Observation, and Intervention
Nominal Group Technique

11. **Questioning Techniques**

    Open- and Closed-Ended Questions
    Socratic Method
    The Importance of Being Nonjudgmental

12. **Project Management Tools and Techniques**

13. **Communication Channels, Informal Networks, and Alliances**

Module 4: Measuring and Evaluating

1. **Theories and Types of Evaluation**

    Purpose and Benefits of Evaluation
    Measurement Process
    Evaluation Development Issues: Validity and Reliability
    Goal Attainment Methods and Performance-Based Training Evaluation
    Formative Versus Summative Evaluation
    Donald Kirkpatrick's Four Levels of Evaluation
    ROI Methodology
    The Balanced Scorecard Approach
    Meta-Evaluation Methods

2. **Statistical Theory and Methods**

    Use of Statistics
    Measures of Central Tendency (Averages)
    Frequency Distributions
    Measurement Scales, Variables, and Classifications
    Measures of Variance
    Correlation
    Statistical Inference and Hypothesis Testing
    Effect Sizes
    Confidence Intervals
    Appropriate Use of Statistical Information and Data

3. **Research Design**

    Concepts and Issues
    Sources of Measurement Error
    Rights of Human Subjects
    Tools for Problem Identification

Preparation for Research Design Development
Data Collection Methods
Data Storage

4. **Analysis Methods**

Uses of Analyses

5. **Interpretation and Reporting of Data**

Qualitative Data
Visual Display of Quantitative Information
Estimation and Reporting of Error
Synthesis of Data
Communication to Users
Use of Recognized Parameters to Report Information

Module 5: Facilitating Organizational Change

1. **Systems Thinking and Open Systems Theory**

What Is Systems Thinking?
What Is Open Systems Theory?

2. **Chaos and Complexity Theory**

Chaos and Complexity Theory Defined
How Chaos and Complexity Relate to Facilitating Organizational Change
Similarities and Differences Between Chaos and Complexity
OD Intervention

3. **Appreciative Inquiry Theory**

Leading Groups or Teams
Using Effective Questioning Techniques
Integrating Multidisciplinary Learning Topics or Courses
Using Experiential Activities to Expand Learning
Understanding Organizational Realignment

4. **Action Research Theory**

Action Research and Learning
Bloom's Taxonomy
Six Sigma Processes
Kepner-Tregoe
Groups or Teams Facilitation
Meeting Management
Multicultural (Global) Environment Management

5. **Organizational Systems and Culture, Including Political Dynamics in Organizational Settings**

   High-Performance Organizations
   Organizational Structure Models
   Current Culture Benchmarking
   Leadership Models
   Employee Motivation and Productivity
   Role of Top Management
   Cultural Factors at Work With Technology

6. **Change Theory and Change Models**

   Defining the Current State
   Defining Intended Outcomes
   Selling the Change Strategy
   Planning for Change
   Analyzing Stakeholders
   Considering Cultural Implications
   Setting Milestone Evaluations
   Introducing Change
   Overcoming Resistance or Complacency
   Understanding Reactions to Change
   Implementing Change
   Evaluating Effects of Change

7. **Process Thinking and Design**

8. **Engagement Practices to Build Critical Mass**

   Performing a Needs Analysis to Define a Need for Change
   Using Six Sigma Practices for Presenting and Measuring the Effect on Business or
      Performance Before Change
   Communicating Issues to the Workforce
   Considering the Importance of Owning the Process

9. **Communication Theory**

   How Communication Relates to Facilitating Change
   Communication Styles
   Communication Channels, Informal Networks, and Alliances

10. **Diversity and Inclusion**

11. **Motivation Theory**

    Motivation Best Practices

Employee Motivators
Considerations for Motivating Learners

12. **Mindset and Mental Models and Their Influence on Behavior and Performance**

Management Styles
Personal Social Styles
Emotional Intelligence

Module 6: Managing the Learning Function

1. **Needs Assessment Methods and Needs Identification**

2. **Adult Learning Theories**

3. **Learning Design Theory**

4. **Learning Technologies**

   Technology-Based Solutions
   Authoring Tools
   Effects of Different Computer Languages on Instructional Material Development

5. **Learning Information Systems**

   Types of Learning Information Systems
   Learning Management System (LMS) Implementation Overview
   Effects of Learning Information Systems

6. **Marketplace Resources**

   Strategic Advantages of Outsourcing Training
   Vendor Materials
   Off-the-Shelf, Customized, or In-House Development
   Steps in Outsourcing

7. **Basic Understanding of Programs Being Administered**

   Program Administration
   The Role of the Training Manager
   Program Elements
   Trainers
   SMEs (Subject Matter Experts)

8. **Budgeting, Accounting, and Financial Management**

   Strategic Plan Development
   The Role of the Training Manager

Accounting Terminology

Budget Management

9. **Principles of Management**

Training Manager Activities

Functions of Management and Leadership

10. **Project-Planning Tools and Processes**

Project Management

Considerations in Selecting a Project Manager

The Project Life Cycle

Time Management

Project Tools

Project Management Considerations

11. **Communication and Influence**

12. **HR Systems**

Human Resource Systems

Training and Development

Employee-Related Activities

13. **Business Model, Drivers, and Competitive Position**

State of the Business

Culture or Value Systems

Organizational Structure

Knowledge Exchange Network

14. **External Systems**

External Environmental Factors

External Relationships

15. **Legal, Regulatory, and Ethical Requirements**

Employment Law and Regulatory Requirements

Civil Rights

Workplace Safety

Securities and Financial Reporting

IT Compliance

Union Relations

Intellectual Property

Corporate Policies and Procedures

Ethical Standards

16. **Emerging Learning Technologies**

> Strategies for Keeping Current
> Evaluation of New Technologies
> Implementation of New Learning Technologies

Module 7: Coaching

1. **Conduct Standards**

> Role of a Workplace Learning Coach
> Definitions of Coaching
> Criteria for Selecting a Coach
> Issues to Overcome When Coaching

2. **Ethical Guidelines**

3. **Coaching Competencies**

> Setting the Foundation
> Developing Coaching Competencies
> Facilitating Learning
> Measuring Results
> Understanding the Coaching Process
> Identifying Coaching Opportunities
> Using Facilitation Methods and Cognitive Dissonance
> Enhancing Coaching With Technology
> Considering Coaching Certification and Training Programs
> Understanding Mentoring
> Coaching Makes an Unexpected Difference
> The Return-on-Investment of Executive Coaching

Module 8: Managing Organizational Knowledge

1. **Knowledge Management Concepts, Philosophy, and Theory**

> Information Versus Instruction
> Concepts of Knowledge Management
> Elements of Knowledge Management
> Goals of Knowledge Management

2. **Knowledge Management History and Best Practices**

> History of Knowledge Management
> Best Practices

3. **Activities and Initiatives**

   Knowledge Mapping in an Organization
   Purpose of Knowledge Mapping
   Knowledge-Mapping Process
   Key Principles of Knowledge Mapping
   Understanding Corporate Culture and Leadership
   Attitude of Management
   Implementation of the Right Rewards and Incentives
   Means of Capturing Knowledge
   Knowledge Management Support in the Organization
   Effects of Knowledge Management

4. **Understanding Business Processes**

5. **Business Process Analysis**

   Business Process Identification and Discovery
   Various Workflows
   Analysis Tools and Techniques
   Project Management and Project Life Cycle Issues

6. **Technology Enables Knowledge Sharing**

   Overview
   Content Management Systems (CMS)
   Learning Content Management Systems (LCMS)
   Portals and Portal Tie-Ins With Related Sites
   Document Management Systems
   Collaboration Tools
   Requirements

7. **Information Architecture**

   Overview
   Collaboration
   Knowledge Bases
   Systems

8. **Database Management**

   Database Server Platforms
   Query Generation
   Specialists to Support the System

Performance Testing
Support for Specific Formats
Back-Up Facilities and Fall-Back Procedures

9. **System Analysis and Design**

Standard Techniques for Developing Systems

10. **Strategies to Manage Culture Change**

11. **Adult Learning Theory**

12. **After Action Review (AAR) Methodology**

Measurement of Improvement
Lessons Learned Implementing Knowledge Management Systems
Metrics for Usage and Value

Module 9: Career Planning and Talent Management

1. **Workforce Planning Approaches**

Relationship Between Strategic Planning and Workforce Planning
Role of HR in Workforce Planning
Roles of Workplace Learning and Performance Professionals in Organizations

2. **Succession and Replacement Planning Approaches**

Definition of Succession Planning
Job Movement and Replacement Approaches
Approaches to Strategic Plan Integration and Succession Planning
Succession Planning Processes

3. **Job Analysis Tools and Procedures**

Job Analysis Overview
Data-Collection Techniques
Pre-Job Analysis
Job Analysis Methods
Types of Job Analysis: Advantages and Disadvantages
Uses of Job Analysis Outcomes

4. **Career Development Theories and Approaches**

Balance Between Personal Assessment and the Market
Trait and Factor: Williamson's Theory
Ginzberg's Theories
Super Developmental Framework
Personality or Typology

Behavioral Counseling

Edgar Schein's Career Anchors Theory

Issues Associated With Career Planning Theories

5. **Individual and Organizational Assessment Tools, Including Assessment Center Methodologies**

Human Resource Audits

Multi-Rater Feedback

Personality Type

Issues to Consider When Administering Assessments

6. **Ethical Standards and Legal Issues in Career Counseling and Organizational Restructuring**

7. **Career Counseling Approaches**

Career Counseling Overview

Career Counseling Standards

Career Counseling Theory

Career Counseling Methods

Career Development Models

8. **Coaching and Mentoring Approaches**

9. **Performance Consulting Approaches**

10. **Managerial and Leadership Development Best Practices**

Managerial and Leadership Development Overview

Formal and Informal Methods

Types of Adult Learners and Seven Must-Follow Principles of Adult Learning

Need to Train to Meet Competency Gap

11. **Performance Management Systems and Techniques**

12. **Approaches to Maximize Workplace Diversity**

Cultural Awareness

Gender and Race Awareness

Generational Differences

Personal Space

Disability Awareness

Training Implications for Multiple Languages

Inclusion Approaches

13. **Resources for Career Exploration and Lifelong Learning**

    Human Capital
    What's In It for Me? (WIIFM)
    IDPs (Individual Development Plans)
    Informational Interviews
    Job Rotation
    Multiple Modalities for Learning

Appendix B
Readiness Assessment
CPLP Self-Assessment by AOE

To use the following self-assessment by AOE, understand that you will need to evaluate your own expertise level, determine your own gap, and select from a variety of learning strategies to bridge the gap. Following is a matrix for each AOE and includes a listing of the key knowledge areas for each AOE. For each key knowledge area, fill in your level of expertise, whether a gap exists, and what learning strategies you plan on using to address the gap. Use the numerical and letter ranking shown in the rating guide below to help direct your preparation for the CPLP knowledge-based exam. This will give you a good indicator of how much preparation you need relative to a specific AOE. Repeat this exercise with each of the key knowledge areas for all nine AOEs in the material provided.

Expertise and Strategy Rating Guide

Level of Expertise:	Learning Strategy Codes:
1 – No Exposure	(C) = Classroom
2 – Basic Understanding	(E) = Experiential
3 – Moderate or Expert Level Understanding	(R) = Research or Study
	(W) = Web-based Course
	(F) = Facilitated Learning
Gap:	(M) = Mentor or Study Buddy
1 – Need Substantial Development	(I) = Independent Study
2 – Need Some Development	
3 – Need Little to no Development*	
*Review of the material prior to taking the CPLP knowledge exam is still recommended.	

Designing Learning Readiness Assessment

Related Knowledge	Level of Expertise	Gap	Learning Strategy to Address Gap
Cognition and Adult Learning Theory			
Instructional Design Theory and Process			
An Exploration of Instructional Methods			
Various Delivery Options and Media			
Job or Task Analysis and Competency Modeling			
Content Knowledge and Content from SMEs			
Assessment Methods and Formats			
Learning Technologies and Support Systems			
New and Emerging Learning Technologies and Support Systems			
Business Strategy, Drivers or Needs Associated with Possible Learning Interventions			
Research Methods			
Individual, Group, and Organizational Differences that Influence Learning			
Legal and Ethical Issues Related to Designing Learning			
Differences between E-Learning and Traditional Courses			
Design of Information Displays, Access, and Resources			

Level of Expertise:

1 – No Exposure
2 – Basic Understanding
3 – Moderate or Expert Level Understanding

Gap:

1 – Need Substantial Development
2 – Need Some Development
3 – Need Little to no Development*

*review of the material prior to taking the CPLP knowledge exam is still recommended.

Learning Strategy Codes:

(C) = Classroom
(E) = Experiential
(R) = Research or Study
(W) = Web-based Course
(F) = Facilitated Learning
(M) = Mentor or Study Buddy
(I) = Independent Study

Delivering Training Readiness Assessment

Related Knowledge	Level of Expertise	Gap	Learning Strategy to Address Gap
Adult Learning Theories and Techniques			
Instructional Design Theory and Methods			
Instructional Methods			
Training Delivery Options or Media			
Existing Learning Technologies and Support Systems			
Emerging Learning Technologies and Support Systems			
Presentation Techniques and Tools			
Organizational Work Environment and Systems			
Individual Learning Styles			
Cultural Differences			
Familiarity With Content Being Taught and How the Solution Addresses the Need			
Legal and Ethical Issues Relevant for Delivering Training			

Level of Expertise:

1 – No Exposure
2 – Basic Understanding
3 – Moderate or Expert Level Understanding

Gap:

1 – Need Substantial Development
2 – Need Some Development
3 – Need Little to no Development*

*review of the material prior to taking the CPLP knowledge exam is still recommended.

Learning Strategy Codes:

(C) = Classroom
(E) = Experiential
(R) = Research or Study
(W) = Web-based Course
(F) = Facilitated Learning
(M) = Mentor or Study Buddy
(I) = Independent Study

Improving Human Performance Readiness Assessment

Related Knowledge	Level of Expertise	Gap	Learning Strategy to Address Gap
Human Performance Improvement			
Business, Performance, and Gap Analysis			
Root Cause Analysis			
Intervention Selection and Implementation			
Measurement and Evaluation			
Change Management			
HPI Models			
Systems Thinking and Theory			
Group Dynamics Process			
Facilitation Methods			
Questioning Techniques			
Project Management Tools and Techniques			
Communication Channels, Informal Networks, and Alliances			

Level of Expertise:

1 – No Exposure
2 – Basic Understanding
3 – Moderate or Expert Level Understanding

Gap:

1 – Need Substantial Development
2 – Need Some Development
3 – Need Little to no Development*

*review of the material prior to taking the CPLP knowledge exam is still recommended.

Learning Strategy Codes:

(C) = Classroom
(E) = Experiential
(R) = Research or Study
(W) = Web-based Course
(F) = Facilitated Learning
(M) = Mentor or Study Buddy
(I) = Independent Study

Measuring and Evaluating Readiness Assessment

Related Knowledge	Level of Expertise	Gap	Learning Strategy to Address Gap
Theories and Types of Evaluation			
Statistical Theory and Methods			
Research Design			
Analysis Methods			
Interpretation and Reporting of Data			

Level of Expertise:

1 – No Exposure
2 – Basic Understanding
3 – Moderate or Expert Level Understanding

Gap:

1 – Need Substantial Development
2 – Need Some Development
3 – Need Little to no Development*

*review of the material prior to taking the CPLP knowledge exam is still recommended.

Learning Strategy Codes:

(C) = Classroom
(E) = Experiential
(R) = Research or Study
(W) = Web-based Course
(F) = Facilitated Learning
(M) = Mentor or Study Buddy
(I) = Independent Study

Facilitating Organizational Change Readiness Assessment

Related Knowledge	Level of Expertise	Gap	Learning Strategy to Address Gap
Systems Thinking and Open Systems Theory			
Chaos and Complexity Theory			
Appreciative Inquiry Theory			
Action Research Theory			
Organizational Systems, Culture, Politics			
Change Theory and Change Models			
Process Thinking and Design			
Engagement Practices to Build Critical Mass			
Communication Theory			
Diversity and Inclusion			
Motivation Theory			
Mindset, Mental Models, and Their Influence on Behavior and Performance			

Level of Expertise:

1 – No Exposure
2 – Basic Understanding
3 – Moderate or Expert Level Understanding

Gap:

1 – Need Substantial Development
2 – Need Some Development
3 – Need Little to no Development*

*review of the material prior to taking the CPLP knowledge exam is still recommended.

Learning Strategy Codes:

(C) = Classroom
(E) = Experiential
(R) = Research or Study
(W) = Web-based Course
(F) = Facilitated Learning
(M) = Mentor or Study Buddy
(I) = Independent Study

Managing the Learning Function Readiness Assessment

Related Knowledge	Level of Expertise	Gap	Learning Strategy to Address Gap
Needs Assessment Methods and Needs Identification			
Adult Learning Theory			
Learning Design Theory			
Learning Technologies			
Learning Information Systems			
Marketplace Resources			
Basic Understanding of Programs Being Administered			
Budgeting, Accounting, and Financial Management			
Principles of Management			
Project-Planning Tools and Processes			
Communication and Influence			
HR Systems			
Business Model, Drivers, and Competitive Position			
External Systems			
Legal, Regulatory, and Ethical Requirements			
Emerging Learning Technologies			

Level of Expertise:

1 – No Exposure
2 – Basic Understanding
3 – Moderate or Expert Level Understanding

Gap:

1 – Need Substantial Development
2 – Need Some Development
3 – Need Little to no Development*

*review of the material prior to taking the CPLP knowledge exam is still recommended.

Learning Strategy Codes:

(C) = Classroom
(E) = Experiential
(R) = Research or Study
(W) = Web-based course
(F) = Facilitated learning
(M) = Mentor or Study Buddy
(I) = Independent Study

Coaching Readiness Assessment

Related Knowledge	Level of Expertise	Gap	Learning Strategy to Address Gap
Conduct Standards			
Ethical Guidelines			
Coaching Competencies			

Level of Expertise:

1 – No Exposure
2 – Basic Understanding
3 – Moderate or Expert Level Understanding

Gap:

1 – Need Substantial Development
2 – Need Some Development
3 – Need Little to no Development*

*review of the material prior to taking the CPLP knowledge exam is still recommended.

Learning Strategy Codes:

(C) = Classroom
(E) = Experiential
(R) = Research or Study
(W) = Web-based Course
(F) = Facilitated Learning
(M) = Mentor or Study Buddy
(I) = Independent Study

Managing Organizational Knowledge Readiness Assessment

Related Knowledge	Level of Expertise	Gap	Learning Strategy to Address Gap
Knowledge Management Concepts, Philosophy, and Theory			
Knowledge Management History and Best Practices			
Activities and Initiatives			
Understanding Business Processes			
Business Process Analysis			
Technology Enables Knowledge Sharing			
Information Architecture			
Database Management			
System Analysis and Design			
Strategies to Manage Culture Change			
Adult Learning Theory			
After Action Review (Methodology)			

Level of Expertise:

1 – No Exposure
2 – Basic Understanding
3 – Moderate or Expert Level Understanding

Gap:

1 – Need Substantial Development
2 – Need Some Development
3 – Need Little to no Development*

*review of the material prior to taking the CPLP knowledge exam is still recommended.

Learning Strategy Codes:

(C) = Classroom
(E) = Experiential
(R) = Research or Study
(W) = Web-based Course
(F) = Facilitated Learning
(M) = Mentor or Study Buddy
(I) = Independent Study

Career Planning and Talent Management Readiness Assessment

Related Knowledge	Level of Expertise	Gap	Learning Strategy to Address Gap
Workforce Planning Approaches			
Succession and Replacement Planning Approaches			
Job Analysis Tools and Procedures			
Career Development Theories and Approaches			
Individual and Organizational Assessment Tools, Including Assessment Center Methodologies			
Ethical Standards and Legal Issues in Career Counseling and Organizational Restructuring			
Career Counseling Approaches			
Coaching and Mentoring Approaches			
Performance Consulting Approaches			
Managerial and Leadership Development Best Practices			
Performance Management Systems and Techniques			
Approaches to Maximize Workplace Diversity			
Resources for Career Exploration and Lifelong Learning			

Level of Expertise:

1 – No Exposure
2 – Basic Understanding
3 – Moderate or Expert Level Understanding

Gap:

1 – Need Substantial Development
2 – Need Some Development
3 – Need Little to no Development*

*review of the material prior to taking the CPLP knowledge exam is still recommended.

Learning Strategy Codes:

(C) = Classroom
(E) = Experiential
(R) = Research or Study
(W) = Web-based Course
(F) = Facilitated Learning
(M) = Mentor or Study Buddy
(I) = Independent Study

Appendix C
Common Pitfalls

Like any other skill, successfully passing the Work Product submission is a competency you need to develop. Please read over these tips based on observations made during the pilot program, conducted in 2005-2006.

Pitfall	Impact	How to Avoid	Tip	Example
Candidate did not provide sufficient evidence; candidate evidence was sparse or superficial.	Candidate received low scores.	Provide examples; remember the burden of proof is on you. Review examples of completed sample forms.	Provide some examples; don't always just provide narratives but use facts or examples to support your explanations and conclusions.	If you are showing outcomes, for example, provide some examples of why your project was so successful or had the impact it did.
Candidate chose a Work Product that was wholly inappropriate, provided no evidence, or completely irrelevant information.	Candidate received a zero and failed the Work Product submission.	Make sure you read through the scoring guidelines, key elements, and selection criteria carefully before choosing your Work Product.	As a general rule, if you can comfortably address the key elements and scoring guidelines, you should be in good shape. If it's a stretch, consider choosing another project.	An example of an inappropriate submission was a literature review. The raters could not apply the rating guidelines and there was no basis for the raters to score the project.
Candidate mislabeled or did not clearly label evidence in Work Product.	Candidate received a low score or a zero because the raters could not identify specifically where the proof was located	Be explicit on Form A and identify the location of all key elements in your Work Product – you need to clearly direct the raters to it! If possible, use a time and date stamp when you make the recording. That way you know for sure the raters are seeing exactly what you specify.	The rater's job is not to search far and wide for evidence. Imagine if you were there in the room with the rater, and telling them what to look for – You need to be very clear.	
Candidate did not thoroughly answer the follow-on questions. Candidates misinterpreted follow-on questions.	Candidate received a low score or sometimes a zero.	Do not zoom in on one part of the follow-on question at the expense of another. Do not provide an answer that ignores critical aspects of the follow-on question.	Address all parts of the question fully.	

Pitfall	Impact	How to Avoid	Tip	Example
Candidate provided a Work Product that was not within the past three years.	Candidate received a zero score.	Make sure to submit a recent project. If the project is in progress, make sure there is enough substantive work already completed.	Ask yourself: Do I have enough information to pass the outcomes section? Sometimes a work in progress does not allow you to provide evidence of impact.	
Candidates did not understand how the scoring guidelines were being used.	Candidate submitted a Work Product that was deficient.	Education. Know that the raters use the scoring guidelines to rate Part 1 of your Work Product. You want to pay particular attention to these guidelines.	Know that these guidelines are used heavily, but they are not exhaustive. They are NOT treated like a checklist. You do not have to show everything in every area to receive a passing score. But you must demonstrate enough to show the rater that you are competent.	
Candidate assumed that the Work Product raters know who they are, their reputation, or their background and experience and that this knowledge will weigh into the scoring process favorably.	Candidates risk losing points for failure to provide details or sufficient information!	Provide clear and thorough responses to questions. Identify locations of all evidence of the key elements. Read and re-read your submission to ensure that you've given enough information.	Read your responses aloud or let your family members read your responses to see if they are thorough and clear. Remember that these are blind submissions. The raters are looking for you to demonstrate your expertise.	
Candidates used poor grammar or gave garbled responses.	Garbled responses risk being misinterpreted by the raters, resulting in a lower score.	Have you read messages where grammatical errors and poor sentence structure caused you to lose your concentration? Make sure that what you want to say is well articulated.	Read your responses and descriptions aloud.	
Candidates submitted sloppy, poorly copied, or messy Work Products.	The candidates risk that the rater will not understand what they are trying to convey, thus resulting in a lower score.	Review your Work Product carefully before submitting it. Recopy anything that is unclear, use paper that is uniform in size for your various forms, etc.		Candidates occasionally submit Work Products where pages do not fully print and do not catch the mistake before submitting the project.
Candidate waits until the last minute to prepare responses to the	Follow-on questions are worth one-third of the score. Candidates can easily lose	Treat your follow-on questions as test questions with the same level of importance as	Read the tips in the Candidate Bulletin on how to approach the follow-on questions.	

Pitfall	Impact	How to Avoid	Tip	Example
follow-on questions.	enough points on the follow-on questions to cause the Work Product to fail.	the rest of your Work Product.		
Candidate waits until the last week before the deadline to begin the Work Product!	Candidates submit a Work Product that's below par or incomplete.	Plan ahead. Review the guidelines. Start early.	Know what is needed and plan enough time to complete your Work Product!	
Candidate does not check to see if your submission will play or is audible.	Some Work Products had to be returned, without being scored.	Make sure your Work Product meets the technical guidelines that are outlined in the Candidate Bulletin.	Check to make sure you Work Product submission will play back on a different machine other than the one where you recorded it.	

Appendix D
Work Product Timeline

Use this checklist to help guide your process of submitting your Work Product. Remember that some of the items may take more time, depending on your schedule and workload.

Weeks to deadline	✓	Work Product Preparation
12		• Receive notification that you passed the knowledge-based exam. • Review your work project history for the last three years and determine the best project to submit as your Work Product.
11		• Begin collecting materials and documents to submit in support of your Work Product. • Strategize how you will present those materials in a reader-friendly manner for Work Product scorers. • Due to the time-intensive nature of collecting signatures, begin to obtain participant signatures for the Work Product Release Document.
10		• Write a first draft summary description of your Work Product for the Work Product Submission Form. • Begin to identify the location of evidence of key elements in your Work Product for the AOE core components—project relationships, plans, outputs, and outcomes—on the Work Product Submission Form.
9		• Create your first draft answers to the eight questions specific to your AOE for the Work Product Supporting Evidence. • Finish locating evidence of key elements in your Work Product for the Work Product Submission Form.
8		• Continue to obtain signatures for the Work Product Release Document. • Review your summary description and make necessary updates, edits, and changes. • Review and edit your draft answers to the Work Product Supporting Evidence questions.
7		• Begin drafting your answer for Follow-On Question 1.
6		• Receive comments from your volunteer reviewer and make any necessary amendments to your summary description or answers to the Supporting Evidence questions. • In addition, begin drafting your answer to Follow-On Question 2.
5		• Make any necessary adjustments to your answers for Follow-On Questions 1 and 2.
4		• Ensure that you have obtained all necessary signatures for the Work Product Release Document. In addition, complete the Identification and Contact Information.
3		• Begin to organize your Work Product for submission, following the guidelines in the Candidate Bulletin at www.astd.org/astd/cplp/cand_bul.htm. • Reread your summary description and review indicators of key elements (Work Product Submission Form); examine your answers to the eight questions (Work Product Supporting Evidence); review your answers to Follow-On Questions 1 and 2. Make any necessary edits.
2		• Organize your Work Product package for submission. Take time to ensure that materials are labeled correctly and that scorers will find it easy to navigate through your Work Product materials.
1		• Submit Work Product package.

Appendix E
Subject Matter Expert Consultants

In order to ensure content accuracy and instructional design integrity, the *ASTD Learning System* was reviewed by a diverse group of professionals in the field. Each subject matter expert provided the *ASTD Learning System* development team with invaluable feedback and advice regarding the content of each module.

ASTD would like to extend a special thanks to Elaine Biech, who volunteered a considerable amount of her time and effort to review the *ASTD Learning System* in its entirety. We are extremely grateful for the hours and hours she spent working with us to ensure we delivered the best possible product.

Elaine Biech is president of ebb associates, an organization development firm that helps organizations work through large-scale change. Biech has been in the training and consulting field for 26 years working with business, government, and not-for-profit organizations. She has presented at dozens of national and international conferences and has been featured in dozens of publications, including *The Wall Street Journal, Harvard Management Update,* and *Fortune.* She specializes in helping people work as teams to maximize their effectiveness. She facilitates topics such as coaching, fostering creativity, customer service, speaking skills, training competence, conducting productive meetings, managing change, handling difficult employees, and communication. She is the author and editor of dozens of books and over a thousand articles, including *Training for Dummies,* 2005; *Marketing Your Consulting Services,* 2003; *The Consultant's Quick Start Guide,* 2001; *Successful Team-Building Tools,* 2001; *The Business of Consulting,* 1999; *The Consultant's Legal Guide,* 2000; and the *ASTD Sourcebook: Creativity and Innovation,* 1996. Her books have been translated into Chinese, German, and Dutch. Biech is active at the national level of ASTD, serving on the National ASTD Board of Directors, initiating and chairing Consultant's Day for seven years, and as the International Conference Design Chair in 2000. In addition to her work with ASTD, she has served on the ISA and ICA boards. Biech is the recipient of the 1992 National ASTD Torch Award and the 2004 ASTD Volunteer-Staff Partnership Award. In 2001 she received The ISA Spirit Award. She has been the consulting editor for the prestigious Training and Consulting Annuals published by Jossey-Bass/Pfeiffer for the past 10 years.

Module 1: Designing Learning

Chuck Hodell is deputy provost of the National Labor College in Silver Spring, Maryland. He is also on the adjunct faculty of the University of Maryland Baltimore County (UMBC) in the graduate program in instructional systems development. He has a PhD in language, literacy, and culture from UMBC, where he also received his master's degree in instructional systems development. His undergraduate degree is from Antioch University, The George Meany Center for Labor Studies. A second edition of his ASTD Press book, *ISD From the Ground Up: A No-Nonsense Approach to Instructional Design*, will be published in 2006.

George Piskurich is an organizational learning and performance consultant specializing in e-learning interventions, performance analysis, and performance management. His workshops on self-directed learning, structured mentoring, instructional design, facilitation skills, and preparing learners for e-learning have been rated "outstanding" by participants from organizations world wide. With more than 25 years of experience in learning technology, he has been a classroom instructor, training manager, CLO, instructional designer, and e-learning and performance consultant for multinational clients and smaller organizations. He has been a presenter and workshop leader at more than 30 conferences and symposia, and is an active member of both ISPI and ASTD. He has written books on instructional technology, facilitation skills, self-directed learning, instructional design, and telecommuting, authored journal articles and book chapters on various topics, and has edited three books on e-learning. In 1986 he was ASTD's Instructional Technologist of the Year, and recipient of the Best Use of Instructional Technology in Business award in 1992.

Module 2: *Delivering Training*

Jean Barbazette is president of The Training Clinic, a training consulting firm she founded in 1977. Her company specializes in train-the-trainer, new employee orientation, and enhancing the quality of training and instruction for major national and international clients. Her degree from Stanford University is a master's degree in education. She is the author of the best-selling book, *Successful New Employee Orientation*, Jossey-Bass/Pfeiffer Publishers. She has authored three training packages: *Customer Service: Back to the Basics, Telephone Techniques,* and *Dealing with Difficult Customers*. Her second book, *The Trainer's Support Handbook*, was published by McGraw-Hill in 2001. Her book, *Instant Case Studies*, was published by Jossey-Bass/Pfeiffer in 2003. Her new book *The Trainer's Journey to Competence: Tools, Assessments and Models*, was published by Jossey-Bass/Pfeiffer Publishers in 2005 and is the first volume in *The Skilled Trainer Series*. Additional books in *The Skilled Trainer Series* are *Training Needs Assessment* and *The Art of Great Training Delivery*, which will be published in 2006. She is a frequent contributor to several Pfeiffer Annuals.

George Piskurich (See Module 1: *Designing Learning* above.)

Module 3: *Improving Human Performance*

Mason Holloway has an extensive professional background, including 17 years in senior management and consultative positions working in business consulting, business operations, sales, and human performance improvement (HPI). He has demonstrated skills and expertise in assisting organizations in meeting and exceeding aggressive and competitive organizational goals and improving overall business results through HPI processes. His clients have included Dell, the U.S. Navy, National Technical Information Service, L.L. Bean, the Social Security Administration, Accelera Corporation, ServiceMaster, ADP, and Microsoft. He went on to found and develop a nationally recognized publishing company, serve as digital content delivery consultant to a major content provider, and work with a team developing a contextual learning management system for the U.S. government, among other achievements. Working with partner Dennis Mankin, Holloway led the design and development team in the creation of Performance DNA, the most comprehensive and effective toolset for analyzing human performance. Performance DNA has been co-copyrighted by Platinum Performance Group and ASTD and is the only methodology taught in the prestigious HPI certificate program. He has taught the Performance DNA approach to hundreds of individuals across the United States and internationally. He is an expert in the methodology, and his facilitation style and knowledge have made him a sought-after instructor, advisor, and project consultant. Holloway graduated from University of Maryland with a bachelor's degree in English and business and continued graduate studies in management at James Madison University.

Karen McGraw is the president of Cognitive Technologies, a high-performance project services firm that delivers complex, mission-critical projects on time and on budget. She has extensive experience in technology-based performance improvement solutions, ranging from the design and implementation of computer-based learning and learning management systems, to expert systems, performance support systems, intelligent interfaces, and knowledge management systems. She is a co-developer of the Performance DNA toolkit for analyzing human performance to diagnose improvement opportunities. She also was a co-developer of the Human Capital Capability Scorecard, a unique system that measures the factors that affect an organization's ability to profit from human capital development and management initiatives. She is nationally recognized in performance analysis and design, e-learning, knowledge acquisition, and scenario-based requirements, and has authored five texts, including *User-Centered Requirements* and *Knowledge Acquisition: Principles and Guidelines*. She has written more than 35 articles and is a frequent presenter at industry conferences, such as ASTD TechKnowledge and the Conference Board, speaking on topics such as e-learning strategy, human capital development and optimization, change management for new technologies, and competency-based performance management. McGraw received her doctorate from

Texas Tech University in educational psychology and curriculum and instruction, specializing in the cognitive and performance effect of technology. Postgraduate training includes organization development, change management, performance engineering, knowledge engineering, software engineering, and leadership. McGraw is a member of ASTD and ISPI.

Module 4: *Measuring and Evaluating*

Malcolm Conway is an IBM-certified business transformation managing consultant with IBM's Business Consulting Services Public Sector Human Capital Management practice. His expertise is in improving and measuring organizational, team, and individual performance to achieve business results. He improves and manages performance through learning and other interventions; designs, manages, programs, and conducts organizational assessments; designs and manages the implementation of electronic and mail surveys and data collection; designs and manages the implementation of skills management systems, including coaching and mentoring; and measures change. An experienced project and program manager, he has successfully managed a variety of large, medium, and small projects, and is the recipient of an IBM Director's Award for outstanding project management. He has also taught preparation courses for professional certification in project management. Conway facilitates business strategy development and develops learning strategies for instructor-led training and e-learning; designs and manages certification testing programs; designs and manages performance measurement systems; analyzes and improves business processes; designs, manages and evaluates learning programs; designs and evaluates hard-skills and soft-skills curricula and manages and delivers training. He consults in the defense and public education (K–12, higher education) areas of the private sector. His cross-industry experience is in multiple industries and sectors, including telecommunications, manufacturing, retail, pharmaceutical, financial services, IT, transportation, utilities, health care, hospitality, entertainment, and transportation.

Donald V. McCain is founder and principal of Performance Advantage Group, an organization dedicated to helping companies gain competitive advantage through the development of their human resources. With more than 30 years of corporate and consulting experience, his focus is on design and development of custom learning experiences in leadership, sales and marketing, call center management, and many areas of professional development that result in improved business unit and individual performance. He also consults in human resources development (HRD) processes, including design and development, competency identification and development, certification, evaluation (including transfer and ROI), presentation and facilitation, and managing and marketing the HRD function. Most of his clients are Fortune 100 companies across various industries. His work is international in scope. He has also consulted with many "new consultants" on the business side of training consulting. He has a BBA in marketing and economics, M. Div., MBA in HR and marketing, and an EdD in HRD from Vanderbilt University. In addition, he is currently a visiting professor at the School of Business, Tennessee State University; and former adjunct professor for the School of Management, Belmont University. McCain also teaches for the University of Phoenix and was an adjunct assistant professor of Leadership and Organizations for Vanderbilt University. He is author of the book *Creating Training Courses (When You're Not A Trainer)*, *Evaluation Basics*, and co-author of *Facilitation Basics*. He also wrote the lead article for *HRfocus*, "Aligning Training With Business Objectives," and has published several evaluation instruments.

Jack Phillips is a world-renowned expert on measurement and evaluation and chair of the ROI Institute, which provides consulting services, workshops, and keynote addresses for Fortune 500 companies and major organizations around the world. His expertise in measurement and evaluation is based on more than 27 years of corporate experience in five industries. Phillips has served as training and development manager at two Fortune 500 firms, senior HR officer at two firms, president of a regional federal savings bank, and management professor at a major state university. He developed the ROI Methodology, a revolutionary process that provides bottom-line figures and accountability for all types of training, performance improvement, human resources, and technology programs and is used worldwide by corporations, governments, and not-for-profit organizations. He is the author or editor of more than 30 books and more than 100 articles. His most recent books are *Proving the Value of HR: How and Why to Measure ROI* (SHRM 2005), *Investing in Your Company's Human Capital: Strategies to Avoid Spending Too Much or Too Little* (AMACOM 2005), *ROI at Work: Best-Practice Case Studies From the Real World* (ASTD Press 2005), *Return on Investment in Training and Performance Improvement Programs*, 2nd Edition (Butterworth-Heinemann 2003), and *The Human Resources Scorecard: Measuring the Return on Investment* (Butterworth-Heinemann 2001). Phillips earned his doctorate degree in human resource management.

Patricia Pulliam Phillips is president and CEO of the ROI Institute. She earned her doctoral degree in international development and her master's degree in public and private management. Early in her professional career, Phillips was a corporate manager who observed performance improvement initiatives from the client perspective and knew that results were imperative. As manager of a market planning and research organization for a large electric utility, she and her team were responsible for the development of electric utility rate programs for residential and commercial customers. In this role, she played an integral part in establishing Marketing University, a learning environment that supported the needs of new sales and marketing representatives. Internationally known as an accountability, measurement, and evaluation expert, she facilitates workshops all over the world and consults with U.S. and international organizations—public, private, not-for-profit, and educational—on implementing the ROI

Methodology. Phillips is the author of *The Bottomline on ROI*, (CEP Press 2002), which won the 2003 ISPI Award of Excellence. She is editor or co-author of *ROI Basics* (ASTD 2006), *ROI at Work: Best-Practice Case Studies From the Real World* (ASTD Press 2005), *Proving the Value of HR: How and Why to Measure ROI* (SHRM 2005), *The Human Resources Scorecard: Measuring the Return on Investment* (Butterworth-Heinemann 2001), and *Measuring ROI in the Public Sector* (ASTD 2002).

Module 5: *Facilitating Organizational Change*

Jeff Russell, co-director of Russell Consulting, specializes in helping organizations achieve great performance internationally while successfully responding to the challenges of continuous change. With a focus on leadership, strategic thinking, leading change, and performance coaching, he has worked with organizations as diverse as Fortune 500 firms, social and public sector organizations and small, family businesses. He received his master's degree in industrial relations from the University of Wisconsin-Madison where he serves as an ad hoc faculty member for Wisconsin Certified Public Manager Program; the Small Business Development Center; and the UW campuses of Madison, Milwaukee, and Green Bay. Russell is a frequent presenter at local, national, and international conferences. Most recently he presented at the 2002, 2003, 2004, and 2005 International Conferences, the 2004 Jamaica Employers Federation Convention, the 2004 and 2005 Wisconsin State SHRM Conference, the 2005 National Conference of the American Society for Public Administration, and the 2005 Minnesota Quality Conference. Russell and his wife and business partner Linda have co-authored six books: *Managing Change; Managing the Problem Employee; So, You Want to be a CEO?; Leading Change Training* (ASTD Press 2003); *Strategic Planning Training;* and, most recently, *Change Management Basics* (ASTD Press 2006). Articles on their leading change model and their research on employee resilience have appeared in Wiley's Pfeiffer Annual in 2005 and 2006. They also publish the workplace learning journal *Workplace Enhancement Notes*.

Carol Ann Zulauf has her own consulting practice, specializing in leadership, team development, and systems thinking. Her clients span high tech, federal and state governments, health care, education, and consumer product organizations. She is also associate professor at Suffolk University in Boston, having co-designed the master's program in adult and organizational learning. Prior work experience includes being a senior training instructor for Motorola. Zulauf has many publications to her credit, including the newly published book by Linkage, *The Big Picture: A Systems Thinking Story for Managers*, and is a frequent presenter at regional, national, and international conferences.

Module 6: *Managing the Learning Function*

Jean Barbazette (See Module 2: Delivering Training.)

Bob Rosania is a nationally recognized training and career development professional with more than 25 years experience working with individuals and organizations to improve performance, manage change, and develop effective career management strategies. He currently serves as a senior career management consultant with Jewish Employment and Vocational Services in Philadelphia, where he provides individual and group consulting services. Previously he was a vice president and career management consultant at Manchester. He has also served as a senior principal at The Touchstone Partnership and was the director of human resource Development at ARAMARK Healthcare Support Services Division. He is the author of two books: *Presentation Basics* and *The Credible Trainer* and was a major contributor to the book *Improving Performance in Organizations (In Action Series)*. He has appeared as a guest on the CNN televised Your Morning Show, as well as on a number of Philadelphia radio programs speaking on career development and work-life balance issues. Rosania has also presented at numerous national meetings, including ASTD, The Training Directors Forum, and The American Dietitian Association, and serves as a Board member and volunteer for Joseph's People, a not-for-profit organization providing support to the unemployed. He has a master's degree in student personnel services in higher education (counseling) from Seton Hall University and a bachelor of arts degree in Psychology from the University of Dayton.

Lou Russell is CEO of Russell Martin & Associates, a consulting company that designs and delivers learning experiences that are fun, fast, flexible, and measurable and specific to unique problems. She has served as a consultant to companies, schools, and colleges to help each grow their own organizational ability to learn. Her first book, *The Accelerated Learning Fieldbook*, is a comprehensive resource that helps accelerate learning in business and educational settings. Her second publication is *Project Management for Trainers* (ASTD Press). This book is based on actual experiences in her consulting work, including applying project management to a global medical products sales conference, an Internet technology curriculum, safety training, as well as project management for fourth graders. Her third book, *IT Leadership Alchemy*, focuses on the criticality of technical leadership. Based on several research projects, it addresses how successful leadership is the result of using one's formal role and personal abilities to motivate and influence others to move toward a specific business goal. Russell focuses her fourth book, *Leadership Training* (ASTD Press) on leadership in the middle of organizations. It includes a CD with material for a half-day, one-day, or two-day class. In October 2005, she published another book, *Training Triage* (ASTD Press) *that* provides emergency remedies for the real training challenges and situations most professionals face every day. Russell is also the editor of the electronic monthly newsletter *Learning Flash*. She speaks nationally at conferences, such as ASTD, Training, Project Management Institute, and ProjectWorld.

Module 7: *Coaching*

Chris W. Chen is an organizational change and process improvement manager with Sempra Energy, a Fortune 500 company in San Diego. He also runs his own consulting business, specializing in leadership training. He has led the training and development function for several San Diego companies. He has been a program manager for the Center for Creative Leadership, as well as a line manager in the finance, human resources, and information technology functions. He has a bachelor's degree from the University of California, Irvine in Economics. His master's of business administration is also from UCI, with an emphasis in organizational behavior. Chen was an adjunct professor of organizational behavior at California State University, Long Beach, and lectured on TQM at the John Anderson Graduate School of Management. He has published four books, *Simply Spoken Leadership, New Supervisor Training, Coaching Training,* and *The Big Book of Six Sigma Training Games.* He has also published articles on a variety of human resource topics and been quoted as a management expert by *The Washington Post* and *Chicago Tribune.*

Jennifer Long is senior vice president of program development for The Source International, Australia's number one company in executive skills development and a global leader in skills and performance coaching. Long has spent 18 years with the company in training design, production, and the co-development and refinement of its proven coaching methodology. She also heads the design and production of all company technology-based learning solutions to complement the proven courses currently instructor-based. Long has incorporated her expertise in directing, improvisation, and production into the dynamic interactive learning that has become the hallmark at The Source and has developed learning programs for British American Tobacco, AT&T, United Artists, Ford Motor Company, and Northrop Grumman. She is currently working on the ongoing development of the national network of Source Certified Master Coaches that supports the company's instructor- and web-based coaching services. She produces a quarterly global newsletter, writes and contributes articles to industry trade publications, and manages global marketing efforts as well as public relations. She remains passionate about keeping the experience of the Source as dynamic, real, and personally beneficial as possible.

DJ Mitsch is a master certified coach, one of the first 25 designated by the International Coach Federation (ICF). As the 2001 president of the ICF, she led the association across borders to become recognized as the global professional society of coaches and served on the board of directors for six years as the ICF developed the certification programs and the ethics and standards for coaching. Mitsch founded The Pyramid Resource Group, The Corporate Coaching Company, in 1994 with her life and business partner Barry Mitsch. Her client list includes the world's largest telecommunications companies, pharmaceutical companies, real estate investment firms, high-tech innovators, medical not-for-profits, broadcasting companies, retail organizations, and professional sports organizations. The teams Mitsch coaches achieve extraordinary business goals through a proprietary program, The Extraordinary Game. She has written culture changing coaching initiatives for in-house organization development teams to teach coaching skills to managers. Some of these initiatives are featured in the book, *Coaching for Extraordinary Results*, published by ASTD in 2002. Prior to entering the coaching field, Mitsch had a stellar 16-year career as a broadcast executive. Responsible for operations, sales, administration, finance, marketing, promotions, and facilities construction, she consistently reported to a chairman and board of directors in her executive roles.

Module 8: *Managing Organizational Knowledge*

Ralph E. Grubb is an industrial/organization development psychologist and was a pioneer in instructional technology and performance improvement at IBM's Thomas J. Watson Research Center, Yorktown Heights, New York. He held a number of technical management positions for IBM in educational research, technology, and personnel research in the United States and Europe. During recent years, Grubb has been a consultant to Motorola University and IBM on instructional program design, development, and evaluation of customer programs; KPMG for more than 45 technical projects ranging from program evaluation, instructional design, development of curricula for the consulting and information risk management practices, advanced statistical analysis of organizational surveys, project management course development and consulting, performance-based project management job aids, to the design of an award-winning national distance learning network and program involving 51 remote sites; and the Office of Technology Assessment of the U.S. Congress for analyzing training and performance in the workplace. Grubb completed his doctorate in psychology and education at Teachers College, Columbia University and has been adjunct professor of education there for more than a decade. He has served on the Board of Trustees for both the Graduate School of Education and Human Development at the University of Rochester, and the Regents College, the University of the State of New York, Albany. He has authored more than two dozen publications on the topics of performance improvement

Lisa Haneberg is a management consultant and acclaimed author and expert in personal and organizational success, organization development, management and leadership training, and human resources. She offers both integrated training solutions and individual and group coaching. Her first book, *High Impact Middle Management: Solutions for Today's Busy Managers* was a groundbreaking and practical tool for professional middle managers. She has also written *Organization Development Basics* and *Coaching Basics* for ASTD Press. She also wrote *Focus Like a Laser Beam* and was one of 11 contributors to the book, *More Space: Nine Antidotes to Complacency in Business*, a collection of essays written by some of the brightest minds and freshest voices in business. Haneberg reaches a worldwide audience through her popular blog, Management Craft, which offers resources and perspectives to leaders, managers, and those who develop and coach them. During a business career that has spanned more than two decades, she has worked with leaders at all levels and for many types and sizes of organizations, including high-tech manufacturing (Intel); distribution, manufacturing, and services (Black & Decker, Mead Paper); e-retailing and distribution (Amazon.com); travel and leisure products and services (Beacon Hotel, Travcoa, and Cruise West); and the Royal Government of Thailand. She is a certified master trainer and behavioral assessment interpreter. She earned an undergraduate degree in behavioral sciences from the University of Maryland and has taken graduate courses at Johns Hopkins University and Ohio State University.

Michael Marquardt is professor of human resource development and program director of overseas programs at George Washington University. He also serves as director of the Global Institute for Action Learning. He has held a number of senior management, training, and marketing positions with organizations such as Grolier, ASTD, Association Management, Overseas Education Fund, TradeTec, and the U.S. Office of Personnel Management. He has trained more than 95,000 managers in nearly 100 countries since beginning his international experience in Spain in 1969. He is the author of 18 books and more than 90 professional articles in the fields of leadership, learning, globalization, and organizational change, including *Optimizing the Power of Action Learning, Leading with Questions, Building the Learning Organization* (selected as Book of the Year by the Academy of HRD), *The Global Advantage, Action Learning in Action, Global Leaders for the 21st Century, Global Human Resource Development, Technology-Based Learning,* and *Global Teams.* More than one million copies of his publications have been sold in nearly a dozen languages worldwide. Marquardt also served as the editor of the UNESCO Encyclopedia volume on human resources. Marquardt's achievements and leadership have been recognized though numerous awards, including the International Practitioner of the Year Award from ASTD. He currently serves as a senior advisor for the United Nations Staff College in the areas of policy, technology, and learning systems.

Module 9: *Career Planning and Talent Management*

Steve Merman began his career as a professor of counselor education at the University of Colorado, but left academia to build a successful consulting practice that achieved recognition at the local, regional and national levels. As a way to round out his experience, he served as manager of human resource planning and development for Amoco Production Company as a well as a faculty member with Amoco's Management Learning Center. He has held numerous leadership positions with ASTD and co-authored selected ASTD Press publications on career management systems and assessments. Merman is a member of the International Coaching Federation and holds the PCC designation from that organization. He is also certified as a co-active coach with the Coaches Training Institute. He travels internationally to enjoy trekking opportunities in Africa and Asia and is an avid snowshoe enthusiast and cyclist.

Annabelle Reitman has more than 30 years experience in career coaching and counseling, specializing in resume development targeting clients' professional stories and short-term coaching for clients in career or professional transitions and changes. She is an established writer for online and print publications and author of three books. Her latest publication is *High-Level Resumes: High-Powered Tactics for High-Earning Professionals* (Career Press, 2005). Her doctorate and master degrees in higher education administration are from Teachers College, Columbia University.

The *ASTD Learning System* development team would also like to thank the following for being available to us and offering their expertise around the clock: **Bruce Aaron, Paul Bernthal, Stella Cowan, Elizabeth Hannah, Stew Hickman, Sharon Kimble, Tom LaBonte, Michelle Lavoie, Jennifer Naughton, Donna Richey-Winkelman, and Ethan Sanders.**

ASTD Learning System Editorial Staff

Director: Cat Russo
Manager: Mark Morrow
Editors: Tora Estep, Jennifer Mitchell

Contributing Editors
April Davis, Sabrina Hicks, Stephanie Sussan

Proofreading
April Davis, Eva Kaplan-Leiserson

Graphic Design
Kathleen Schaner

ASTD (American Society for Training & Development) is the world's largest association dedicated to workplace learning and performance professionals. ASTD's 70,000 members and associates come from more than 100 countries and thousands of organizations--multinational corporations, medium-sized and small businesses, government, academia, consulting firms, and product and service suppliers.

ASTD marks its beginning in 1944 when the organization held its first annual conference. In recent years, ASTD has widened the industry's focus to connect learning and performance to measurable results, and is a sought-after voice on critical public policy issues.

Thomson NETg Staff

Solutions Manager: Robyn Rickenbach
Director: John Pydyn

Contributing Writers
Lynn Lewis, Dawn Rader:

Contributing Editors
Lisa Lord, Kim Lindros, Karen Day

Thomson NETg is a global enterprise-learning leader offering an integrated suite of learning modalities and content, next generation technologies, and supportive strategic services designed to align with key organizational initiatives. NETg clients ensure continual, enterprise-wide acquisition of knowledge and information while lowering the overall cost of learning for the organization. With the KnowledgeNow Suite, clients are able to develop, customize, host, deliver, and report on engaging learning initiatives, delivered in blended modalities. Thousands of leading companies and government agencies around the world rely on Thomson NETg to achieve important business productivity and performance improvements. From healthcare to telecommunications, manufacturing to pharmaceuticals, retail to financial services, military operations to human services, NETg KnowledgeNow consistently delivers.

NETg is backed by The Thomson Corporation, a global enterprise comprised of a vast array of world-renowned publishing and information assets in the areas of academics, business and government, financial services, science and health care, and the law.